MARKETING ON THE INTERNET

Marketing, Selling, Business Resources on the Internet

MARKETING ON THE INTERNET

Working the Web Series

Simon Collin

B.T.BATSFORD LTD LONDON
Batsford Business Online: www.batsford.com

© Simon Collin 1999
First published 1999

Simon Collin has asserted his
moral right under the Copyright,
Designs and Patents Act, 1988, to be
identified as Author of this Work.

Published by:
B.T.Batsford
583 Fulham Road
London SW6 5BY, England

Batsford Business Online: www.batsford.com

Printed by
Whitstable Litho
Whitstable
Kent

ISBN: 0 7134 8551 5

A CIP catalogue record for this book
is available from the British Library

CONTENTS

Dedication

To

Francesca, Natasha and Nicolas - a great team!

INTRODUCTION

AT the start of the Internet revolution, no one thought of using the medium as a part of a marketing strategy. The online world was basic, mostly academic and totally unsuitable for the ways of marketing departments. However, the Internet developed astonishing quickly and within a few years it was proclaimed as the business revolution. Entrepreneurs made millions with virtual products that only existed in the ether. Then the marketing revolution arrived and with it a barrage of bad publicity.

Some of the first companies to use the Internet to market products had a field day. They had a captive, untapped audience of tens of millions of users and could utilise a whole range of promotional tools. It is unfortunate, then, that many of the early campaigns were executed with little regard for the medium, its users and their pro-active tendency. As a result, the first people to send out millions of unsolicited email adverts were thrown off the Internet. It has taken all the efforts of good marketing orginizations to restore the name of direct email techiniques.

In this book, I cover the Internet from the marketing point of view. I have tried to cover all the ways of using the power of the different parts ot the Internet within your marketing strategy. Most importantly I also explain how the different techiniques work, how to implement them and the results that you can expect.

The first chapter is included as a general introduction ti the Internet and how it works. This provides the basic groundwork that allows me to explain how the different features and functions are implemented. The rest of the book is arranged by different topic, from advertising to measuring response, design through to press relations.

Online marketing is fast becoming not only a new opportunity, but for many techniques it provides the most efficent system available. As an example, in the case of working with the press and in direct marketing, email must be the future of these branches of marketing. It provides an immediate, very low cost system that delivers direct to the user's desk. In the case of brand marketing, the two sides are undecided. And with advertising, perhaps the heyday of the web-based advertising is over and agencies realise that traditional print advertising is just as effective and often cheaper. I cover these topics, the arguments for and against and the ways of using types of online marketing.

The one certainty is that you cannot ignore online marketing. With its wide reach and effects, it is now an essential ingredient in any complete marketing strategy. In this book, I set out to provide you with a resource of ideas, practical techniques and contact details to help you use the Internet for an effective marketing strategy.

Simon Collin, 1998
simon@workingsite.com

CHAPTER 1

An Introduction to the Internet

THE Internet is one of the most important developments in business communication and computing; if you ignore the benefits and potential of the Internet, you will lose a considerable commercial advantage. The Internet lets you market and sell your products to a pool of more than 100 million potential customers.

This book does not try and provide a comprehensive guide to getting online. Instead, it concentrates on how to make use of the resources on the Internet. This chapter provides a basic introduction to the different parts of the Internet and explains what you will need to get online and help you understand your options and so make the best choice.

What is the Internet?

The Internet is made up of thousands of separate computers, called servers, that are linked together. These servers are linked using high-speed communication channels (similar to a telephone cable) that allow information to flow from one computer to the next. Each of these servers has a unique identifying number, called its IP address, but for the sake of user-friendliness, these complex numbers also have a corresponding text label called the server's domain name.

Each of the servers that makes up the internet can do several things. They can pass on information destined for another server and so act as one link in passing a message from A to B. They can also respond to simple commands and can send information or files when asked. Almost all the features of the internet are supported using these two functions (see box)!

> **Two commands to control the web**
> Most of the features of the Internet work very simply and are achieved with little processing power - only the newest multimedia features require serious computing power on the web server. For example, if you send an email message, it is transferred as a file passing from one server to the next until it reaches the correct destintion. Each server just checks the destination address and passes it on. The web pages in a web site are stored as files with all the text and images formatted using special commands (called HTML commands – see Chapter 3 for more details). When a user types in the address of a site on her web browser, the browser sends a simple command to the web server asking it to send back the file that contains the web page. The user's web browser decodes the instructions and displays the page.

To work on the Internet, you need to connect your desktop or laptop computer to the Internet. What you will actually do is link your computer to one of these servers and use this as a soapbox from which you can shout commands to other servers on the Internet. To link to a server, most people use an Internet service provider (ISP) company. These companies own one of the servers that are part of the Internet and link their computer to the public telephone system using a bank of modems. If you have a modem and an account with the Internet service provider, you can dial their number and connect to their server over the standard telephone system. I cover this aspect of the Internet in detail later in this chapter.

The world wide web

The best known part of the Internet is probably the world wide web (also called the www or web). Developed as a working concept by Tim Berners Lee, the web is the reason the Internet has become so popular. The best way to visualise the web is to draw a parallel with a vast library. The building of the library is the Internet, the server computers that fetch the books and provide information are the librarians. The web is based around web sites (the same concept as a book); a web site is a self-contained unit owned and run by an organization or person and contains dozens, hundreds or thousands of individual web pages. Each web page can include images, text, video clips, sound, and animation.

The last part of this concept model is the most important – it's called hyperlinks. A hyperlink allows one item (it can be a word or image) to contain a link to another web page. If a user clicks on the linked item, they are whisked off to the new page. If you have a web page with a list of cars for sale in a showroom a user can click on the name of the car and the hyperlink will send them to the individual page that has all the details for this car. On the details page, there is the address for the showroom – if they click on the address, they jump to a new page that displays a map of the area.

If you want to publish your catalogue on to the web, you would create separate pages for each item. The main index page (called, in internet-speak, the index page!) would have links to each product together with separate pages for ordering, contact details, outlets and so on. More complex sites would have web pages for discussions, trouble-shooting, product updates, company news, press-rooms and so on.

To access the web, you'll need a connection to the Internet and a web browser. To see how these elements work together, see later in chapter.

Electronic mail

The most widely used part of the Internet is electronic mail (email). Email allows you to send a message to any other user who is connected to the Internet – for a minimal cost. Once you have a connection to the Internet and email software, you can write and send messages to any other user. How email works and how to configure your desktop, laptop or office network for email is covered later in this chapter.. The messages are reliable, delivered directly to the recipient's computer and you can even ask for an automated receipt to confirm that the user has received and read your message.

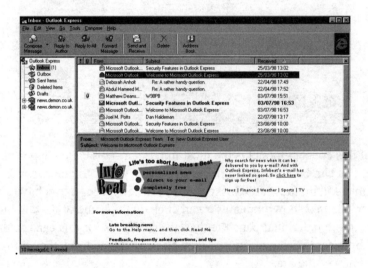

Email cuts through the irritation of voicemail and the delays of postal service and allows the sender to communicate when they want and allows the recipient to read and reply to the messages when convenient. It is cheaper than a fax or postal service and very convenient.

In fact, one of the problems of email is that it is a victim of its own success. Many users are now suffering information-overload and receive several hundred messages per day. The other problem is that, because it is so easy to send a message, most people do not think about their message content before sending it. Emails are often ruder, blunter and less polite than any other form of communication. You would never dream of making a joke in a fax to a customer, but many people add jokes and smiley faces to their business email correspondence!

Email is also used to great effect to provide discussion groups and distribute newsletters. If a person wants to create a discussion group about growing orchids, they could setup a mailing list and invite other interested users to join the list. Any messages sent to the list are distributed among all the members of the list. Similarly, a newsletter can be sent to thousands of subscribers by email with no postal or production costs and instant delivery. Chapters 3 and 7 cover this in detail.

Email in marketing has taken off – you can now distribute your press releases to thousands of reporters via email agencies (see Chapter 10 for more information). Direct email – sending unsolicited advertising messages – has a poor reputation, but carefully targeted direct email (to users that have said that they are ready to accept advertising by email) is revolutionising the direct mail system. Chapter 10 covers this in detail.

Newsgroups

Newsgroups provide an online discussion forum that, collectively, is often referred to as the Usenet. There are more than 20,000 newsgroups covering everything from programming to direct marketing, business travel to teaching methods. Anyone can join a newsgroup and read or post messages using newsreader software.

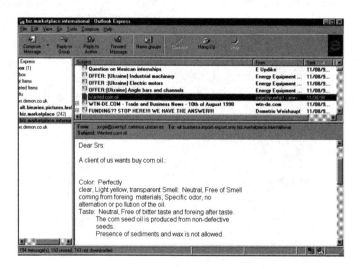

Newsgroups are one of the most active parts of the Internet – with hundreds of thousands of new messages posted every day. By comparison, the content of the web changes very little. Newsgroups provide a good opportunity for a company to promote its expertise rather than flaunt its products. You should monitor the newsgroups that cover your company's product range and answer occasionally and intelligently. If a user wants to complain, they can do so to best effect in a newsgroup! Also, users ask for opinions, technical support and recommendations in newsgroups.

I have covered newsgroups in two chapters of this book: when promoting your web site, you should monitor relevant newsgroups and reply when appropriate (see Chapter 4 for more details on promoting your site). When researching a new project, you can use the newsgroup to ask for feedback or to hear what users want (see Chapter 11 for more information).

Get connected

The first hurdle you will have to cross is how to get online. This has become far easier with the introduction of new software and features under *Windows 95* and *Windows 98*. The Windows operating system now includes all the software you need to get connected. However, you should make sure that you understand how each process works and provides a link in the overall service. Over the next few pages, you will see what extra equipment and software you will need to link your computer or your network to the Internet.

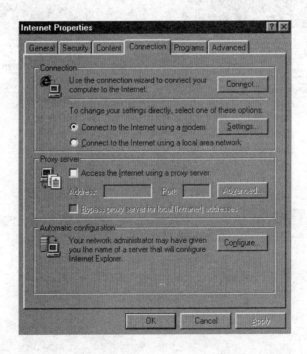

In order to use the Internet, you will need to link your up computer. There are many different ways of linking your computer and this depends on your requirements, office configuration and budget.

Modems

The simplest and cheapest method of getting started is to connect one computer to the Internet using a modem. A modem sends computer data along a standard telephone line and can be fitted either inside your PC or Macintosh or outside to your computer's standard serial port. Laptop, handheld and PDA computers can use PC-card modems that look rather like a fat credit card and fit into a special slot in the computer. External modems that connect to your computer's serial port are more expensive, but are easier to transfer from one computer to another.

Modem technology is always changing to try and improve the transmission speed – that defines how much data can be sent over a telephone connection. The faster modems are more expensive – the current top standard is called 56K (or V.90). To keep up with these new developments, make sure that your new modem has a Flash-memory feature. This will let you upgrade the modem (often for no charge) by simply connecting to the manufacturer's web site and downloading special software.

If you are working from home or in a small office, you might use the extended features provided with many high-end modems, including voicemail that works as an electronic answering machine for normal incoming voice calls.

ISDN

One of the most convenient methods of linking a small office or group of computers to the Internet is to use an ISDN link. You will need to rent a new high-speed digital telephone line (the ISDN line) – installed by your telephone provider. To connect your computer to this new telephone line you will need the digital equivalent of a modem – called an ISDN adapter. It is about the same price as a high-end modem but can transfer information more reliably and faster. ISDN adapters are available as either internal or external units and can fit into standard PC and Macintosh computers – there are also PC-card ISDN adapters to use with a laptop.

One of the best features of ISDN is that calls are made almost instantly. When you try to get online using a normal modem, it will take almost one minute to dial the number and connect. ISDNcompletes this process in under one second! This gives you the impression of near-instantconnection and, in a busy office, saves a lot of frustration.

Once you have installed an ISDN connection, you will find that web pages are displayed more quickly and files are much faster to download (see panel on speeds and response times). You can still receive and place normal telephone calls over your ISDN line by connecting a telephone handset to your ISDN adapter.

The running costs are a little higher than a normal modem-telephone line setup: installing andrenting an ISDN line is often more expensive than a standard telephone line, but ISDN calls are charged at around the same price as a standard phone call.

Connecting a network

If you have a group of users connected to an office network, it makes sense to connect the network to the Internet and so allow all the users shared access. If there are just a couple of users or you only want email support (rather than web browsing), you can install a shared modem. This modem connects to one computer on the network (typically the server, but it could be a powerful workstation); the computer runs special modem-sharing software that allows any user to access the modem as it were their own. The drawback of this system is that although the modem is shared, only one user at a time can use it. Products such as Artisoft iShare (*www.artisoft.com*) provide modem sharing functionality.

For larger workgroups in which several users want to browse the Internet at the same time, an ideal solution is a shared ISDN adapter. You can setup a shared ISDN adapter in just the same way as a shared modem, but the more common solution is to use an ISDN router. This plugs directly into your network (rather than connecting to a server computer). The router part of the unit automatically detects when any user tries to access the Internet and instructs the ISDN adapter part to dial and provide a connection. Because ISDN can dial and connect in less than a second, the user thinks that they have a permanent link rather than an instant on-demand link. The second major advantage is that many users can use the ISDN router at the same time.

Lastly, if you have a large network or if you have your own in-house web server, then you are likely to use a permanent leased line. This is rented on a yearly basis from your telephone company and provides a very high-speed, permanent connection to the Internet. There are no per-minute connection charges, but the yearly rental is high.

Summary:

1. If you want to connect one computer to the Internet for general browsing, use a high-speed modem.
2. If you want to connect one computer to the Internet with better performance or if you manage your web site, use an ISDN adapter.
3. If you want to link two or three users to the Internet for basic email and browsing, using a shared modem.
4. If you want to link a small network of users to the Internet and allow more than one user to connect at any time, use an ISDN router.

5. For very large company-wide networks or if you have an in-house server you might consider a leased-line

Software required

To use the Internet, you will need to install and configure special software that can manage each part of the process. This is made easier by Microsoft Windows (versions 95 and 98) that includes all the basic software you need to use the Internet.

Essential software

To use the Internet, your computer needs to connect to your ISP or OSP. A utility program – normally called a dialler – will control the modem, dial the telephone access number and connect to the remote computer automatically. You will need this basic software in addition to the rest of the software described in the next sections. Once you have configured this dialler with the telephone number of your Internet company (either an ISP or OSP) the dialler will automatically start whenever you start an Internet application – such as a web browser.

Most Internet providers will supply you with a CD-ROM of setup software; this normally configures the Microsoft dialler utility with the correct access number and installs customised web browser, email and newsgroup software. The two main OSPs – CompuServe and AOL – take a slightly different approach. They wrap up the basic utilities within their own custom, integrated package. It's easier to use than standard Internet software, but is not always quite as flexible.

Electronic Mail Software

To send and receive electronic mail you will need to install email software that works with your Internet provider. Any new mail messages are temporarily stored at your Internet provider's computer; your email software connects to the Internet provider and downloads any new mail messages. At the same time, it sends any messages that you have composed. Unless you have a permanent leased line link to the Internet, you have to check if there is any new mail – it is not automatically delivered to your desktop. The simplest way to provide a regular update is to set your email software to check and exchange new messages on a regular basis – perhaps every hour.

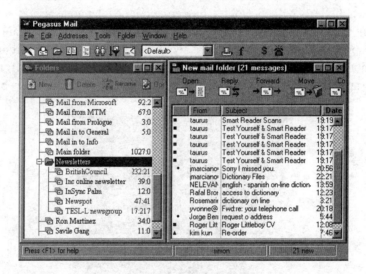

If you are using a stand-alone computer and you do not need to integrate your network email with Internet email (see next section) then you can use one of the dozens of standard Internet email applications. The most popular internet-only email products include Qualcomm's Eudora *(www.qualcomm.com)*, Microsoft Outlook Express *(www.microsoft.com)* and Netscape Communicator *(www.netscape.com)*. All three of these products are available in free versions that can be downloaded from the company's website.There are also plenty of other good email products, many are listed in online shareware libraries such as *www.shareware.com.*

Email standards
There are three main standards used in electronic mail sent over the internet: POP3 and SMTP are used to send and read mail messages and form the basis of almost all internet email products. If you are buying email software to link to the Internet, check that the software does support these standards. The third standard, IMAP4, is new and gaining popularity; if you want to make sure that your email software supports the future, check that it has support, or planned support for IMAP4.

If you are using *Windows 95* or *Windows 98*, you should also have the Microsoft Internet Explorer CD-ROM. This includes Microsoft's *Internet Mail* and *Outlook Express* products that provide a good starting point for internet mail. *Microsoft Office 97* includes the more sophisticated Outlook application that combines email with groupware features

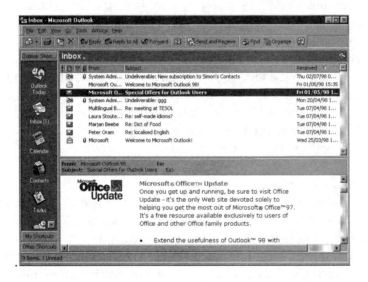

The main OSPs, including CompuServe and AOL, provide their own custom software that lets you send and receive mail messages; you can sometimes use standard internet software with these services, but it is often easier to use the customised products.

Email software is now just as sophisticated as many wordprocessing packages. You can format the text in your message, add images or sound. Email works well as a way of distributing information you can send files using the attachment feature – or maintain a distribution list of email addresses that are used to receive a form message, just like an old fashioned printed mail-merge.

Most email products now provide a folders feature. This works just like the folders under Windows or on a Macintosh; you can organize incoming messages by storing them in different folders. Automatic rules can check incoming messages and move them into the correct folder based on a set of rules that you have defined. For example, you can set up a rule to move all mail from key members of a project into one project folder. More sophisticated rule systems allow you to send an email message with a query, perhaps a stock query, that is then processed automatically and returned to you with the answer.

Lastly, email is very useful within a workflow installation. With more advanced products, you can define a list of users; your original message travels from one user to the next in order and each user is asked to approve or comment on the contents. The message and all the comments are then returned to you.

Network email

If you are using a network email system, such as Lotus cc:Mail or Microsoft Mail, you will have a central server that works as a main postoffice in your office. This can be connected to the Internet using a gateway – special software that works with the postoffice software to allow it to exchange messages with the Internet.

If you are considering adding electronic mail to your network, you have plenty of options! The cheapest is to use the Pegasus email software that will link to the Internet and work on an internal network. Other free products include Microsoft Outlook – but this only supports internet mail unless you buy and install Microsoft Exchange Server. Commercial products including Lotus Notes and Microsoft Exchange provide a combination of network-based groupware, email and links to the Internet.

How email works

Every user has a unique email address. It is made up of two parts, separated by an '@' symbol. For example, my email address is *'simon@workingsite.com'*. The word to the left of the '@' is my name that is unique within the company name (called the domain name) that is on the right of the '@'. If there were two people called Simon Collin at the domain *'workingsite.com'* then one would have to change his email address to differentiate. The combination of your user name and the domain name forms your unique email address.

A domain name is made of two parts: the first part is the company name and the last section is the country name. US companies normally use '.com', UK companies normally use '.co.uk', other countries use similar suffix notation, for example Australia is '.co.au'. Others suffix characters include '.org' for general organisations and '.net' for network providers.

If you connect to the internet using a home-user type account with an internet provider, then you will usually have an email address that has your user name and the domain name of the internet provider. For example, my email address with the OSP CompuServe is 'SimonCollin@compuserve.com'. All CompuServe users have the same domain name.

Free electronic mail
There has been a lot of interest in free email accounts – a service provided by many of the major web sites. These let you set up a new email address that is totally free. Any email messages sent to your free address can either be automatically forwarded to another email address or stored until you read them using a web browser. There's no real catch in this setup - the services are paid for using advertising and if you send mail from your free account, it will contain a short line advertising the service, but it is very low-key.

In order to access a free email service, you still need access to either the web or an internet account. Free email is great if you can only access the Internet through an internet café, or if you want to separate work and home mail. Some of the services include *www.bigfoot.com*, *www.hotmail.com* and *www.yahoo.com*. A new concept available in some countries is the totally free ISP. In the UK one new service is Freeserve *(www.freeserve.co.uk)*

To give your company a more professional look, you should register your own company domain name. For example, if you work for Steel Girders Ltd, you could have an email address at CompuServe of 'SteelGirders@compuserve.com' but it is far more professional to have your own domain such as 'steel-girders.co.uk' – your email address would then be 'mike@steel-girders.co.uk' or similar. To register your own domain name is very easy – and relatively inexpensive. You can ask your ISP to do this for you or you can do it yourself by visiting the '*www.internic.org*' website. (Note that CompuServe and AOL users cannot have their own domain name, they will have to switch to an ISP.) See chapter 8 for more details on domain names and branding.

When another user sends you an email message, they enter your full email address. The main computer at their ISP looks up the domain name and checks the route the message must travel. The message travels over the Internet to your ISP's computer. It is stored temporarily in your account until you use your email software to dial and connect to the ISP and retrieve the message.

If you specify the wrong email address, it will bounce – that is it will be sent back to you with a message that it cannot be delivered. Check the spelling of the user name, the punctuation and the domain name – it's easy to enter a comma instead of a period within the address!

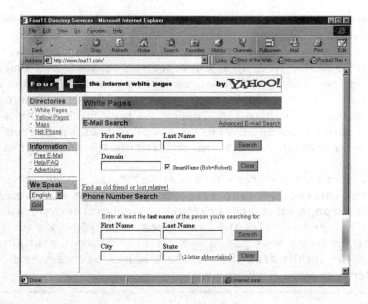

Lastly, if you need to find someone's email address, you can use one of the online white pages services that attempt to list user names and email addresses. They do not list everyone, but it is a good place to start. Visit *www.four11.com* and *www.yahoo.com* to search their address books.

Telephone and fax by email
One of the neatest uses of the Internet is the Jfax service provided at *www.jfax.com*. For a modest monthly fee, you get a unique telephone number in a city of your choice, in the country of your choice. Anyone call telephone this number and leave a voice mail, or send a regular fax to the number. These are then converted into email messages and forwarded on to your nominated email address. It's a perfect way of having a virtual office around the world!

World Wide Web
The reason that the Internet has become so popular is because of the world wide web – normally called the Web or WWW. The web is a collection of millions of pages of information stored on computers around the world. The reason that the web is so popular is because it is very easy to use. Each page on the web can contain text, images, sound, video clips and animation – just like a multimedia book on a CD-ROM.

One of the best features of the web is that it provides a way of linking information between pages. These hyperlinks let you move around between related pages. For example, if you visit a page about classic cars, there might be a list of makes of car – click on Ferrari and the hyperlink will automatically display a new page about Ferraris.

To view a page, you will need to use a program called a web browser. This will convert the special codes used to create a web page and displays the formatted text and images. Moving around web pages and using hyperlinks is called 'browsing' or 'surfing'. However, before you can start browsing the pages on the www, you will need to get connected to the Internet and sign up with an internet service provider (see earlier in this chapter). just like a multimedia book on a CD-ROM.

When you start your web browser, it will check to see if you are currently connected. If you are not, it will automatically start the software that dials up and connects to the Internet. Once you have a connection, you can start using the browser.

What makes a web site?
A web page is stored in an individual file on the disk of a remote computer. A web site is a collection of related web pages; for example, the Microsoft web site has thousands of different individual web pages that hold information about its products, tips, and much more. Each web site has a unique name and each web page stored on the web site has a file name. A browser uses the combination of the web site name and the web page file name to display a particular page on the www.

Brands of browser

There are two main types of browser available – from Microsoft and Netscape. There are some differences between the two, but they will both let you look at web pages and browse the web. If you happen to have both types of browser installed on your computer, you might notice that they sometimes display the same web page in a slightly different way, but this does not normally change the way that you use the page.

Microsoft's Internet Explorer is free and is often already installed with Windows 95 or Windows 98; Netscape's Navigator is also available free in its entry-level version. However, most ISPs will supply a web browser together with all the software you need to connect to the web, but check first.

To view a web page, you need to type in the full name for the page into the box in the top left-hand side of the browser, just below the button bar. This full name is called the URL (uniform resource locator) for the web page.

The first welcome page of any web site is normally stored in a file called 'index.html', however you do not normally need to enter this as part of the URL – you only have to type in the name of the web site. For example, if you type in the address 'www.microsoft.com' into your browser, you will see the main welcome page to the web site.

If you click on a hyperlink to move between pages, you will notice that the name of the web page changes to reflect the name of the new web page. For example, if you want to see the main page on the Microsoft web site that covers Word, type in the URL '*www.microsoft.com/word*'.

You might have noticed that the URL is actually split into four parts, the last three are each separated by a dot. The first part of the URL 'http://' is often left off the full address, because the browser can add this automatically, these characters tell the browser that you want to view a web site. The main URL starts with 'www' that identifies that you are look-ing for a web page, the second part tells you the name of the web site or company 'Microsoft' and the third part identifies the type of web site 'com' is commerical, 'net' is used by ISPs. To say the URL, read '*www-dot-microsoft-dot-com*'.

Sometimes, you might see a URL that has numbers in it; in fact the words in all URLs are translated into numbers so that the computers on the Internet can find the correct web site. This translation is carried out by a huge index stored in computers called Domain Name Servers (DNS). These servers hold a list of the text version of the URL and the numer-ical version. When you type in a new URL in your web browser, the browser asks the nearest DNS to translate this into the numerical address. If there's no such URL, you'll see an error message. Otherwise, the browser then tries to make a connection with the web site address specified by the DNS.

Web technology is developing and changing all the time. The standard way of designing a web page is to use HTML commands, but these are rather limited in their scope and are not very good at handling multimedia, video, sound and animation. To give developers the freedom to add new features to their web pages, a system has been developed that allows mini programs, called applets, to be downloaded as a user visits a web site. These programs are normally written to the Java or ActiveX standards and run on your computer. They can be used to carry out a whole range of functions, from home-banking to multimedia presentations – none of which would be possible with standard HTML commands.

When you visit a complex web site that uses applets, your browser will warn you that it is about to automatically download the applet. If you prefer not to download the program (it could contain a virus or be for malicious intent), you can stop the process. Otherwise, the entire process is invisible to the user.

Another method of adding support for complex web page features is by enhancing the capabilities of the web browser. All browsers can be extended using a piece of software called a 'plug in'. These programs are similar to an applet (described above) but tie-in closely with the browser and allow it to display animation, video clips, sound and other multimedia. If you visit a web site that uses a plug-in, you will be asked if you want to download this. Again, if you are not sure about the authenticity of the company sending you the plug-in, you can refuse. However, plug-ins provide an excellent method of keeping up with the newest technology and are essential if you want to listen to live sound or watch video sequences.

It is worth pointing out that all web browsers allow the user (or network supervisor) to set up secrity features that ensure that only authorised web sites are viewed. This can help prevent users visiting time-wasting or offensive sites or help minimise the risk of viruses and fraud.

Choosing an internet provider

In order to connect to the Internet, you need to establish an account with an internet provider. The provider is the middle-step between you and the world-wide network. An analogous example on your desk is your telephone; the provider is British Telecom or Cable & Wireless and the Internet is the telephone network that lets you connect to any other telephone. With the Internet, there are two types of provider, one offers basic functionality, the other adds extra services.

An ISP (Internet service provider) such as Demon, Direct Connection, or Global Internet provide connection service without frills. Their computers work as a gateway between users dialing in using a modem or ISDN adapter and the Internet. The ISPs provide a series of modem and ISDN telephone numbers that you can dial into – these are called POPs (points of presence). Make sure that the ISP you choose has a POP local to you to minimise telephone costs.

Summary of ISP features

- An ISP is often cheaper than an OSP, starting at £10 per month for a basic account. Business accounts and ISDN users will often have to pay more.
- Can register your own domain name for a fee. Either do it yourself using the *www.internic.net* site or ask the ISP to do it for you.
- Some providers are geared to home users and offer custom news and information.
- ISPs can provide high-speed links, including ISDN and leased line for busy office installations.
- Provide business-related services including consultancy, designing web sites, online commerce.
- Make sure that your ISP provides good telephone support.
- If you plan to use electronic commerce or create and manage mailing lists, make sure that the ISP supports these features at a reasonable cost.

An OSP (online service provider) such as CompuServe, MSN and AOL, offer connection to the Internet plus extra information, news and a range of databases only accessible to members. In addition, OSPs normally supply a complete, custom software package that allows you to manage your email, browse the WWW and use the information services available.

OSPs, like ISPs, have access telephone numbers, but they provide better coverage. Most ISPs limit their telephone access numbers (the POPs) to their local country or region. OSPs provide a world-wide network of local telephone numbers. As an example, if you have an account with a US-based ISP and travel to the UK, you will still need to telephone the US access number to retrieve your email. If you have an account with an OSP such as CompuServe, you would call the local UK number and log in as normal.

Summary of features of an OSP

- Often have a world-wide network of local telephone access numbers so are very good for
  travelling. In contrast, an ISP will be centered in one country.
- Normally charge by connect time.
- Supply extra databases of business information, but these will cost extra to view.
- Do not all support ISDN.
- Do not supply business-related web services such as setting up a web site.
- Provide limited web space for private users to design their own web site.
- Cannot normally use your own domain name. You will be limited to using the OSP's own domain name (such as compuserve.com).

Costs and Speeds

There are two main pricing models used for access to the Internet. Some providers charge a flat fee per month, others charge by the time you spend online.

The costs of going online can be divided into capital costs and running costs and vary from country to country. Once you have purchased the hardware (modem or ISDN adapter) required to get online in the UK, you will need to subscribe to an internet provider and pay telephone costs.

OSPs normally charge fixed monthly fees that includes certain usage, but will then charge you by the time you spend online. For a single user, this can be a good deal, but business or multiple users will find it expensive. ISPs charge a fixed monthly fee that normally covers unlimited time. Ensure that the ISP license allows more than one user to use the account. Sometimes you will need to opt for the more expensive business account.

In addition to the monthly charges, you will also have to pay standard telephone charges for all calls to the provider. Some cable TV/telephone companies have their own ISP and provide cheap calls. Free weekend calls schemes or special offers from telephone suppliers do not normally cover internet numbers. In the US, local telephone calls are normally free, so telephone connections charges are zero. In the rest of the world, you usually have to pay for all calls, so long sessions on the web will cost you in telephone call charges.

The speed at which you view the Internet is governed by the speed of your modem and by the number of other users around the world who are also connected at the same time. If you have a very fast modem, you might still have slow response because your internet provider does not have a fast link to the main Internet. Alternatively, if you have a fast modem, and good internet provider you might still get a slow response because the remote computer that you are trying to access is very busy.

Generally, the main reason for slow response is modem speed and number of users on the Internet. You'll get the fastest response when the US is asleep. For example, if you are in the UK, and you access the Internet after 2pm, the Internet slows down dramatically as users in the US start to connect.

Maximising the office potential of the Internet

If you have invested in the equipment needed to link to the Internet, especially if you have linked a network of users, then you will want to find ways of using this technology to save money in general day-to-day office situations. The rest of this book covers ways in which you can promote your business, but here are some pointers to making the most of the technology to save money.

Electronic mail lets you send and receive messages with any other user linked to the Internet:

- Helps you keep in touch with busy colleagues – they can read their mail when they want rather than be interrupted by a phone call.
- You can distribute documents and files to project members quickly and cheaply.
- Email is very cheap to run, just the cost of a local phone call.
- Keep in touch as you travel – you can access your mail from around the world using standard software or via an internet café.

- Use fax forwarding services to setup virtual offices around the world, convert traditional fax messages into emails that are sent on to you (such as *www.jfax.com*).

The world wide web is made up of hundreds of millions of pages of information stored in a graphic, formatted style.

You can:
- Store company-wide information in a protected section of your public website,for example, a company diary or agenda that keeps remote workers organized.
- Minimise support calls by placing information, tips and solutions to common problems on your web site.
- Minimise order processing by promoting online ordering.
- Use web-based telephone technology to save on long-distance phone calls. You'll need a microphone, speakers, sound card and telephone software that works with your web browser.
- Use the Internet for video conferencing - add mini video cameras to your PC and join in.

Security

Security is a sensitive subject, particularly when accessing the Internet. There are many security scares that can alarm potential users, but with sensible precautions these can be minimised. With no protection it is possible, but very unlikely, for a hacker to access your local computer's files if you are connected and using the Internet.

To help minimise any risk, especially when connecting a network to the Internet, make sure that you install network management software. Network management and gateway software can prevent users browsing non-business sites, such as pornographic sites, and can help manage time limits online by length of time or within fixed hours to prevent users browsing for too long.

You should make sure that you install network access control software or hardware – usually in the form of a firewall. A firewall will check each external user as they try and access your network and will stop any unauthorised users – such as hackers – gaining access or viewing your local files. If you have your own web server, you must fit a firewall. If you are installing a router, used to provide shared Internet access, this provides basic firewall features and prevents other Internet users and hackers gaining access to your network.

It is worth remembering that the Internet is not regulated and does contain many viruses. If you view documents or download files or accept plug-ins to your browser, then there is a chance that you will catch a virus that could damage files on your computer or network.

A virus can be attached to any file, particularly programs and wordprocessing files. Ensure that your network server and desktop computers run anti-virus software. A virus can by caught by downloading software. Warn users or prevent users downloading files with network management limits. Ensure that you have a good virus checker application that runs in the background and continuously monitors your network for new virus attacks.

Make sure that your anti-virus software can detect viruses within attached files sent by email. Keep your anti-virus software up to date with the latest viruses by getting regular updates from the manufacturer. Some virus attacks are via rogue web browser plug-ins. Ensure that your web browser security settings only allow authorised plug-ins to be used. Look at the authentication signature that should be supplied by all plug-in developers to make sure that it is what it claims to be.

CHAPTER 2
Marketing on the Internet

THE Internet provides a whole new way of marketing your company, brand or product. In addition to your standard tool-kit of direct mail, display advertising and sponsorship, you now have direct email, your web site, banner advertising, newsletters and many more opportunities.

Throughout the rest of this book, I cover the different ways of using these various marketing tools; how they work, how to use them and how best to integrate them into your plans. This chapter provides an overview to help you work on your marketing plan. Each section summarises a type of marketing activity and shows you new ways of tackling the subject using the internet. At the end of the chapter, I have put together a check-list to help you integrate online marketing with your traditional plans.

Direct marketing

The Internet promises much for direct marketeers – and, for the most part – delivers. Each user on the Internet can be targeted precisely using their unique email address; visitors to your web site can, often, be identified by country and company. Best of all, custom marketing messages can be delivered free, quickly and directly to the user's desktop.

Before you run off to launch a million-piece email-shot, read Chapter 7 and note the warnings. There are horror stories of heavy-handed companies sending out millions of unsolicited messages to promote their products. These schemes almost always backfire and result in thousands of flame or hate mail messages coming back on your company. The Internet is a pro-active channel and users do not like unsolicited trash or 'spam' mail being delivered into their mailboxes.

However, the email model is almost certainly the future direction for direct marketing. How can the traditional postage or courier service compete with a near-instant, free and direct-to-the-desk delivery mechanism?

Reputable mailing list brokers now operate within strict guidelines and ensure that the names and addresses on the lists are 'opt-in' users. This means that the user has signed up or registered or volunteered his email address and has agreed to accept commercial messages about related products. By choosing mailing lists very carefully, and sticking to the basic rules described in Chapter 7, you will find the direct email marketing is fast, efficient and successful.

Plus: great way of reaching a targeted audience with instant, free delivery of your message to their desktop.

Minus: go about it the wrong way and you will damage your company's reputation in an instant.

Requirements: email software, rented mailing list.

Cost: very low, just the cost of renting the list.

Press relations

An exciting new development on the Internet has been the arrival of 'virtual' press agencies. Almost all reporters have an email address, so it takes little imagination to realise that you could, potentially, deliver your press releases to key journalists instantly using email. In fact, many journalists prefer receiving releases by email because it's up-to-date and convenient – they can look at it in their time rather than spend time on the telephone. By using a specialist agency (that charges a modest fee) you can use their email list of bureaux and reporters that are interested in your subject area.

Chapter 10 covers the different ways of improving press relations using the Internet. Sending press releases is just one possibility; you can provide a reporter's room on your web site, where company briefings, historical documents and financial details are available for any reporter doing research.

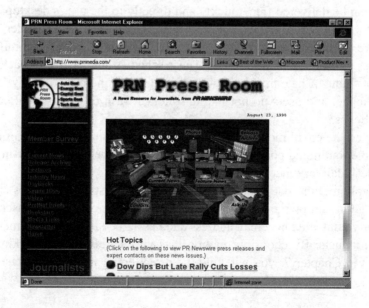

Some of the larger press sites, such as www.prnewswire.com provide private forums that allow reporters to request information – they might be doing a feature about a product or need a case study. By subscribing to these services (as well as monitoring newsgroups, see later) you can make sure that you do not miss any chance to help the press and media and make their job as easy as possible – and so improve your chances of being mentioned in a feature or report.

Plus: helps work better with reporters and delivers your message directly to their desktop.
Minus: make sure you target the right type of journalist for your release.
Requirements: email software, agency fees for delivery.
Cost: minimal costs paid to agency.

Advertising

Using the web as a vast advertising hoarding makes a lot of sense, and many companies are reaping great rewards from the medium. You can advertise through your own site or buy banner advertisements on other sites. The advertising model is near-perfect: choose your niche target audience, find the web site that covers this niche and you have your potential customers. The large, popular search sites (such as Yahoo!) can display a particular advertising message in response to search terms typed in by a user. Now, if you want to advertise a new type of motorcycle gearbox, find motorcycle enthusiast web pages or display your slogan when a user Yahoo! and types in 'motorcycle gearbox'. The advertising response can be measured precisely, since users that click on the banner ad are routed directly back to your web site.

Away from this idyll, there are plenty of industry commentators that note that, on a per-viewer basis, the ad-rates for a tiny banner image on a web site are just as expensive as a full-page, colour ad in a popular magazine.

Plus: exposure to your choice of audience, from niche to general public.
Minus: follow-through response often low, especially for general sites.
Requirements: designer for the banner ad image.
Cost: varies but comparable to a colour magazine advert.

Brand marketing

The Internet is proving to be a great way of carrying out effective brand marketing. Many companies are creating 'virtual' brands that only exist within cyberspace - witness online bookshops, such as Amazon.com, and information providers such as Ziff-Davis (ZDnet). These companies work hard to create an instantly recognizable brand for their web site that might, itself, contain many different affiliated companies.

Creating a new brand on the Internet can be very fast ~ hi-tech internet startup companies grow at fantastic rates and are the current darlings of the venture capital and finance companies. In Chapter 8 I cover the ways in which you can use the Internet to help brand your company or product range. You need to plan carefully, but the basic steps are simple, low-cost and of immediate benefit.

Plus: provide unique information resource that visitors want to visit and use.
Minus: no actual financial rewards and takes a lot of time and effort to maintain.
Requirements: web site design tools, web space, plus related marketing to promote site.
Cost: high startup and running costs in time.

Selling sites

Creating a web site from which to launch a sales-based company can prove a good way of serving your customers. Sites that work towards brand marketing tend not to push a direct selling model and instead provide a resource-based environment, with user feedback, information, news, discussion groups and more.

Sites created for direct sales have to tread a fine line between involving the visitor and yet not geting in the way of a sale. Some sites, such as bookseller *Amazon.com*, work hard to involve the user, making book sales almost secondary, whilst other sites, such as *Download.com* provide direct access to instant software purchases in just a few mouse clicks.

I have not covered the techniques of selling from a web site in this book. These are covered in the companion title *Selling on the Internet* which provides detailed information for companies after a piece of the electronic commerce action – and tells you about transactions, security, processing payments, and delivering products.

Plus: generate revenue, cuts down staff costs, selling direct.
Minus: high costs.
Requirements: need sophisticated web site to support secure selling with shopping cart features.
Cost: very high, long startup time, maintenance high.

Sponsorship

An area that is beginning to provide a great deal of interest is online sponsorship. This generally takes the form of a company paying to have its name linked to a free information source. The Internet started life as a free system that provided information and resources. Many companies are now sponsoring what were originally free sites providing information, this works well in both directions. First, the company is linked with an information rich, philanthropic site that has no other commercial pressures (for example, the Perl programming language site is now sponsored by the O'Reilly & Associates Publishing Company and provides a neat link to its range of books and software that are aimed at Perl programmers.

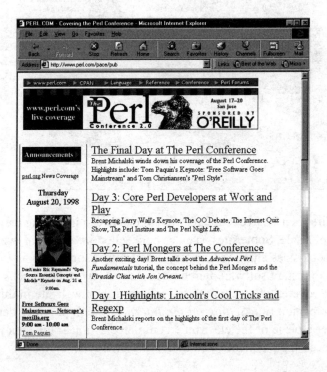

The user gets a benefit in the shape of more money available to the site designers. The site is given a facelift and is brought up to date or enhanced with the sponsorship money. In many cases, where the site was originally run as a hobby, the sponsorship deal ensures that the original author can afford to continue to provide a service.

Plus: promote your brand or site to a new audience that wants the information.
Minus: no control over the content.
Requirements: need a web site where the customer can turn to for more information.
Cost: modest.

Free for the user

Some sites turn the usual model of the Internet as a subscription service concept on its head. For example, many web sites now provide users with a free email address, some provide free web space for a user's home page and some even provide a totally free internet service. The idea is that this promotes the original idea of the Internet as a free information channel.

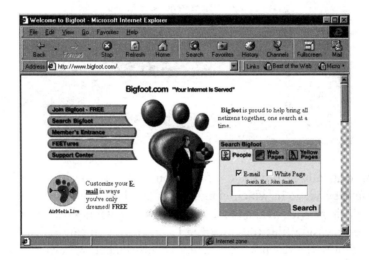

These services are paid for in some way: usually by sponsorship or advertising. For example, Yahoo! (*www.yahoo.com*), Excite (*www.excite.com*), BigFoot (*www.bigfoot.com*) and MSN (*www.msn.com*) all provide users with a free email account, partly as a branding effort and partly paid for with advertising on the site. Sites such as GeoCities (*www.geocities.com*) is funded mostly by advertising and in part by sponsorship to provide users with a free web site, email address and so on. New companies are now starting to provide free ISP services in many countries – funded by advertising – such as Freeserve in the UK (*www.freeserve.co.uk*).

Information delivery services, such as PointCast, InfoBeat and other news channels manage to provide the valuable free news delivery service by including small advertising messages (or large banner ads, in some cases) within each news bulletin.

Response

Without response data, marketing is a guessing game. One of the great features of the Internet is that you can record very detailed information about every person that sees your web site, views your advertisement or reads your marketing emails.

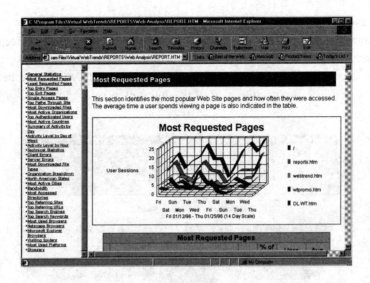

Access logs automatically record basic information about each visitor to your site and notes which web page they view, in which country they are based and, in some instances, their company name. This provides valuable data about your potential customers and their interests. Using these accesslog files (described in Chapter 5), you can follow the response to a marketing campaign or the reaction to a banner advertisement, with exact viewer figures.

By using the sophisticated geo-targeting software (described in Chapter 5), web marketeers can link this information and feedback relevant local-flavour advertisements to the visitors and change their real-world distribution or sales efforts based on this visitor information.

Focus groups for free

The Internet is not just about the web even if it gets all the attention because it looks good and is easy to use. There are plenty of other ways that information is distributed over the internet. One of the most exciting, and the most active, are newsgroups (sometimes called the usenet). These are online discussion forums that cover just about any subject that you can imagine (and plenty that you would rather not imagine).

Any user can join any of the 20,000-plus newsgroups and can read past messages, reply to a message or post a new message. Newsgroups work well because they link together related messages: the original and any replies are all displayed together, making it easy to track a conversation thread. Any user can say anything that they want – and they often do.

This type of forum might sound daunting, but they provide a perfect way of listening to your customers and potential contacts for response to a product (your own or a rival's product). Many of the newsgroups are job or product specific: find the newsgroups that match your company's interests and you can tap in to the opinions and thoughts of your target audience (use search engines such as *www.dejanews.com* or *www.altavista.digital.com* to find newsgroups that match your interests).

In Chapter 11, I explain how you can use the newsgroups for research; plenty of journalists post messages asking for feedback or case-study volunteers. You can also judge the viability of a potential new product by monitoring newsgroups for requests.

Newsgroups are also a good way of implementing a low-key, but often very effective, PR campaign. If you have experts in a particular field, ask them to monitor a particular newsgroup and answer questions authoritatively. Don't turn your postings into an advertising message, instead rely on a short signature at the end of each message to tell other readers about the company. This also works well as a way of de-fusing potential complaints and shows that the company is listening to its customers. These techniques are covered in Chapters 6 and 10.

A second way of distributing information over the Internet is to use mailing lists. These are closed lists of users that have inter-user discussions: messages are sent to the list that then distributes all messages and replies to every subscriber on the list. There are tens of thousands of mailing lists (visit directories of lists, such as *www.liszt.com*) that cover every specialist area imaginable and complement newsgroups. Because mailing lists work via email, any user (even one in a corporation that has email but no direct internet link) can participate.

In Chapter 7, I explain how you can use your own mailing list to distribute information to users, but you can also use mailing lists in the same way that you use newsgroups, to monitor feedback and to provide a low-key PR campaign by contributing and answering other questions.

Planning your online marketing strategy

The key to an effective online marketing strategy is, as in a traditional environment, a good plan. Make sure that you recognise the following points and take them into account when designing your online marketing strategy.

Service

Do more than just an online catalogue; make sure that you provide a real benefit to the visitor, either with information or price or features – ensure that the site is easy to find and use.

Information

Provide depth of information on your site with resource centres, related information, background notes, links to other sites, answers to common questions and news – as well as your product details.

Timely

Keep your site up to date, preferably with a news section or some other feature that is constantly changing and ensures that the visitor will return.

Involvement

Get the visitor involved in your site, either through a discussion group, searchable database, or by providing response forms.

Search Engines

Promote your site for free by spending time indexing your site. Use the techniques described in Chapter 4 to improve your listing in search engine directories.

Direct email

Use this medium carefully and it will show great response; choose your list carefully and make sure that the source opted to receive unsolicited mail. The medium is cheap, instant – beats the postal system any day!

Place banner advertising

Can work well to attract potential visitors to your site. But first, make sure your site is running and is packed with interest! Price can be difficult to justify, since the tiny ad is often the same cost as a large colour magazine ad.

Feedback

Encourage visitors to your site to provide feedback on your company, the service or products.

Global

The majority of internet users are English-speaking, but the rest of the world is a big place! Make sure your information is targeted for a global audience. Consider country-specific sites or pages in different languages; work with local office or your country-specific distributors to provide interest for each group of visitors. Use your response log to check interest by country.

Integrate

Just because you have a web site, doesn't mean you can forget about the rest of your marketing plans! Integrate an email address and the site name into your stationery, print advertising and direct mail.

Participate

The best way to promote your company is by giving good advice for free. Participate on newsgroups with your expert knowledge and leave out the sales pitch – but include a signature with details of your web site.

Work with the press and media

Send out press releases through an email agency, provide reporter rooms on your web site and include company reports, background information, case studies and more to help journalists. Participate in press web sites and newsgroups to listen out for requests from journalists.

Conclusions

This book covers the many new opportunities that you can use to promote your company, news, product, site, brand or expertise. Your strategy will, naturally, depend on your aims; I hope that the many different examples in my book will provide a new set of tools that will help you reach your goal. Even so, perhaps the most important point to remember is that, however exciting, internet marketing should work with existing campaigns and not replace them completely. Online marketing might be (in fact, it certainly is) the future, but the majority of the world is not yet online!

CHAPTER 3
Web site design

BEFORE you create your web site, you should take some time to consider and plan how the site will look and how to make best use of all your resources. The site has to look good and be easy to navigate, but the main point to consider is why you are creating your site. If you are aiming for a site to raise brand awareness, your design should emphasise the brand logo, message and colours. If your site is a selling site, you'll need to provide a quick, efficient route to finding, selecting and paying for a product.

The design elements that you use in your web site will influence the way that visitors respond to the site. In this chapter, I cover the various design issues that are very important when tackling the design of a web site. These design rules are not the same as for printed pages, since the medium is different – the aim is to create a good-looking, informative web site that's easy to navigate, interactive and does not take too long to download and display – the patience of an internet viewer can be measured in seconds!

Within this chapter, I cover sections on how to create an effective web page, how to use colours – both for visual effect and perception and on a technical level – and consider the differences that the visitor's brand of web browser and computer add to the equation.

General design pointers
There are two main problems when designing a Web site. The first is that you are limited to the HTML series of formatting commands. These let you set size and alignment of text and, to a certain degree, you can position images and text on a page using tables and frames (see later in this chapter) but it is still not as precise as with a DTP page layout application. The second problem is one of over-design. If you place lots of graphic images in a printed catalogue, it won't cost you any extra. If you place lots of graphic images on a Web page, you create a lot of data that takes time to transfer and potential visitors will give up waiting for all the images to download.

A simple Web page that has sparing use of line drawings might take just a couple of seconds to transfer and display on a user's computer. A complex Web page with a small photograph and colourful images might take 40-60 seconds. It is possible for users to prevent graphic image being transferred to speed up access to image-rich Web sites, but this rather defeats the point of good design!

To produce a good Web page, you need to think about how the page will look when viewed using different Web browsers (older versions of browsers cannot display some features) and how long it will take to display.

Tips for page content

1. Do not waste your visitor's download time with large graphic images. Use small thumbnails that link to a larger image that can be viewed if the user clicks on the thumbnail.
2. Design for the lowest common denominator; if your design is too restricted with this, at least create a secondary web site that will support simpler, text-based or non-frame based web browsers. There are still millions of users that access the WWW via a text-based browser and won't see images or fancy formatting.
3. Ensure that it's easy to navigate between the pages on your Web site. Try and include a consistent navigation bar on each page.
4. Tell the user if there is new information available or when the site was last updated. No one wants to read old news.
5. Give the visitor a reason to visit your Web site. Will they be able to provide feedback? Can they download a utility or can you provide them with something no other site can?
6. Provide links to other related sites. This proves you know your visitors will look at other sites and that you're making their internet visit a little easier.

Using colour on your pages

When designing your product range and its packaging you will have looked at the impact of choosing different colours. When you design your catalogue, flyer or brochure, you have probably used either corporate or product colours and used the advice of designers or prod-uct marketing professionals in using different colours. The same should be true of the way that you choose colours for the design of your web site. Almost all computers and web browsers can display hundreds and, usually, millions of different colours and hues, so it is worth spending time selecting the colours in your web site carefully.

Colours provide one of the first triggers a customer uses when browsing a shelf for a product; the web is no different. If your web site design uses colour effectively, it will pro-vide an immediate trigger to casual surfers or other visitors to the site.

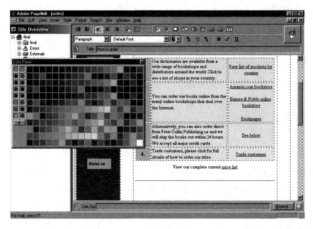

Choosing the best colours for your web site is, unfortunately, not an exact science. Colour experts generally agree that choosing a colour is more often an art than an exact formulae. However, there are plenty of pointers to help you avoid serious mistakes.

What type of colour customer do you have?

Many colour experts divide consumers into three main types according to their reactions to colours. To make your life more difficult, these three types cannot be easily labelled by age, income, gender or race. However, you will know the type of consumer that will buy your product and have a good idea of their reaction to colour.

1. **Adventurous** - these people are adventurous and like new, exciting colours. These consumers tend to be younger and fashion-conscious. They are not necessarily high-income and can be attracted just as well via a fashion magazine as a new brand of ice-cream.

2. **Dependable** - these people are the mainstream consumer group that could, eventually, accept a new colour but only once it has passed from trendy to mass-market.

3. **Scared** - this group of people hate new colours and changes in product design.

Colour by age

You can also divide colour reactions according to age. This is rather easier for children, who generally like brighter, more extreme colours. In boys, an unpleasant colour that they know will upset their parents becomes very appealing – hence the attraction of slime green!

Colour by money

Many consumers will want their products to reflect the fact that it cost a lot. For example, if you have a large and expensive car, sales of models in a bright orange will be poor. Money colours tend to be the more muted white, black, dark green, navy, dark red, grey and silver.

Colour for fun

If a consumer buys a product because they want to use it for fun, or want their peers to think that they are fun, then they will choose brighter colours. If you buy a sports car for the week-ends, and want your neighbours to know that you've got a fun-filled life, you will want it to be bright blue, yellow, or red. Sometimes, with cars in particular, the cross-over point between fun and serious gets muddied. For example, expensive 'serious' sports cars such as a Ferrari would look odd in bright orange. These are serious power cars that deserve power colours such as red, black, dark blue.

Designing with colour

Web designs are still dominated by the idea that a web page is the same as a printed page. As a result, almost all web sites use a white background with black body text as a starting point with the company logo, index and highlights in colour. This actually works well and sites look neat and clean. There is also the advantage that it's easy to read on all types of computer – even those which cannot display colours (such as an older desktop or new handheld or palmtop computer).

The different parts of your web page can each be assigned colours from an almost infinite palette, but these are not guaranteed to display correctly on every type of browser or computer platform. You should stick to the web-safe palette of colours that will display correctly on all platforms. HTML commands allow you to describe the colour of text, background colours to the page or to cells of a table or frame. You can enter these colour control commands manually but, it relies on a number to represent the colour. For more control, use the colour-pick function of a web page design program.

Browser technology

It is a simple fact that not all users have the same web browser – which can be terribly frustrating for a web page designer who is eager to use all the new features of HTML. Try not to create a site that will only work with the latest technology. In many institutions and academic organizations, it's still common for users to be a couple of generations behind the newest version of a web browser. Look at the www.browserwatch.com site for the latest details on types of web browser and statistics that show which browser is most popular with users. At the time of writing, Netscape's web browser still had an estimated two-thirds of the market share, although Microsoft's IE is gaining ground.

Do not forget that most new web browsers also allow users to define how they want the web pages to look. Some users might switch off the graphic image display feature, others might choose a different default font for display.

Size counts

Make sure that you try out your web site with a variety of web browser packages and screen types. Some users have the latest high-resolution video adapters, many are still working at a resolution of 640x480. If your site is promoting a new technology gizmo that will only appeal to cutting-edge computer users – such as web development or programming – then you can be confident that the user will be running the latest versions of the software. If your site is aimed at the general public, go for the lowest-common denominator in terms of gimmicks and site design or your neat tricks will be lost on the majority of your visitors.

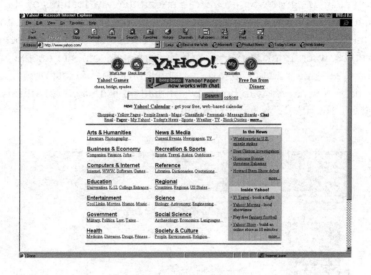

In short, consider the content of your web site first, then turn to the design of each page. Try and cater for users who do not have the latest web browsers and for users who connect via a slow link and so do not want to wait minutes for huge image files.

Compatibility

In the next sections of this chapter, I cover different ways of extending the functionality of basic web page features. This works well to create an impressive site, but tends to only work on certain – newer – web browsers.

If you are developing a web site for developers, there is no problem since you can be sure that the developers will have the latest versions of the web browsers. If, however, you are developing a site for academics or small companies then you might be surprised at the number of universities and schools that have browsers which are two or three releases behind. Large corporate sites might not have the latest browsers installed, as MIS managers wait until the technology is established before rolling it out across the company.

So here's the difficult decision: do you use all the latest techniques to make your site look great to around 5-10 percent of your market, but make it unusable to the other visitors, or do you create two versions of each page that provide the cool version and a simpler version of your site, depending on your client's browser. For any sensible webmaster, the second option is the one to choose! It means more work, in creating a fancy web page and a simpler version, but it will ensure that all your visitors can see the site.

NOTE: Use separate files for new and old browser technology; direct the user to these with a simple opening screen or direct them automatically using a script that detects the type of browser that they are using.

Producing a web page

To start with, a web page is a blank sheet. Any text or formatting that you insert are saved within the page file as HTML markup commands. If you insert an image, the image is actually stored in a separate file, but is referenced by inserting an HTML command in your web page file. Similarly, hypertext links to other web sites or pages are created using HTML commands. (For a complete description of how HTML, web sites and pages work see Chapter 1.)

One web page on your site is normally made up of a several files:
- An HTML file that contains text, formatting commands, references to graphic files and hypertext links.
- Several graphic images stored in separate files. These contain buttons, logo or photographs.

In addition, most sites will also have extra files that support features:
- Database of information that can be searched.
- Sound files.
- Video files.
- Java applets that are downloaded by the user and provide special features such as animation, real-time sound or video playback.
- Program scripts (in Perl or C) that run on the web server and provide a search function, process forms and add other functions to your site.

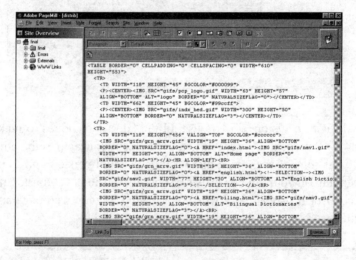

A web page, then, is simply a text file that contains text and HTML commands (they are text-based, such as '<B>' for bold). You can create a web page using a simple text editor, such as Windows WordPad, but it's far easier to use a web page design tool that provides drag-and-drop functionality and hides the (rather off-putting) HTML commands.

The welcome page to any Web site is the first page that is displayed and is usually stored in a file called 'index.html'. The other pages in your site are stored in files with any name you choose (remember that web servers tend to differentiate between upper- and lower-case names). If a visitor enters your domain name in their browser, 'www.MyCompany.com' they will see your welcome page stored in the 'index.html' file. If they enter 'www.MyCompany.com/order.html' then they will see the page 'order.html'.

Web page design tools

At the start of the internet revolution, it was considered macho to type in the raw HTML commands using a basic text editor. Thankfully, attitudes have changed and new page design tools have been developed that give you and your design team the power and flexibility to concentrate on creating complex web page designs without having to understand the HTML commands that form the page.

Good web page design software now has all the features of a desktop publishing product. You can drag and drop graphic elements on to the page, format text by choosing different colours and typefaces from standard menus and align elements. If you have used a DTP or high-end wordprocessing package, these features will all be very familiar to you.

Almost all new web page design tools work on a WYSIWYG (what you see is what you get) method. The page you design is the page that will be seen on the Internet. The design software should also allow you to preview the final page using a standard web browser (such as Netscape or Microsoft IE) to ensure that there are no problems between design and implementation.

There are dozens of different authoring tools that let you create a web page without having to type in HTML commands. The standard authoring package allows you to drag and drop elements on to a blank web page – there are excellent products such as HotDog from Sausage software *(www.sausage.com)*, FrontPage from Microsoft *(www.microsoft.com)*, HoTMetaL (from *www.sq.com*), PageMill *(www.adobe.com)*, Visual Page *(www.symantec.com)*, and NetObjects *(www.netobjects.com)*.

Some of the more advanced applications, such as NetObjects, are designed to work over a company network and allow many different writers and designers to work on the web site at the same time. In larger companies, this type of product ensures that the web site meets every department's requirements and allows the experts from each department to keep their part of the site up to date. Other stand-alone products that do not have this implicit support for multiple users working on one web site can cause problems when updating sites.

The final function of a good web page design program is to help you manage your web site and make it as easy as possible to keep the pages up to date. Many products include site management functions that show you all the graphic files you are using and the relationships between different web pages (the hyperlinks that connect the different pages). It should also provide warnings of missing pages, graphic files or broken links. If you are designing a large and complex web site, then these tools help ensure that all the hyperlinks work and that you are not missing any images. Products such as PageMill, FrontPage, HotDog and NetObjects all provide good site management features.

MICROSOFT FRONTPAGE

Some products, such as Microsoft's FrontPage, provide extra features, called 'bots' that automate complex web page functions such as adding a search engine, creating a form or using animation. However, if you use these FrontPage bots, you must make sure that your ISP supports FrontPage extensions – not all provide this extra functionality.

You will also find that many high-end DTP and office software products provide a feature that allows you to export your work as HTML files. For example, you can use the Corel Ventura DTP software to design a magazine or book, then select Save As HTML and create a near-exact replica that can be published on the internet. Similarly, database products such as Microsoft Access can save selected data files in HTML format, making it relatively easy to create a basic online catalogue.

Using graphics

Graphics are vital – but make sure that you use the same care in design as you do in producing your print or TV advertising. Symbol graphics are used in just about every web site to help navigation, lighten a text-heavy information-rich page or to include images of products or people. Lastly, text can be saved as a graphic image if you want to provide a particular type of formatting that is not possible using the standard (and limited) HTML commands.

The downside of using graphics is that they have to be transferred as the user views the site – if you use too many images, or the files are too big, then the page will take minutes to appear on the user's computer. Remember that internet users have a vast choice of sites and a very short attention span. Many users switch off the 'show graphics' feature of their browser to speed up their surfing, so make sure that your site has text equivalents of images to help users navigate.

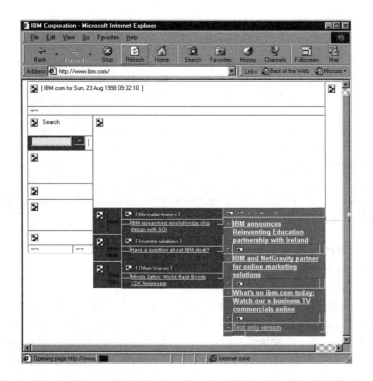

Graphic standards

Most current web browsers support two main image formats that have many differences that makes each suitable for different uses on web pages.

GIF files

do not offer such high quality images as a JPEG image but are usually smaller and so download faster. You can create animated GIF files that cycle a series of images in succession to give the impression of movement – this is how animated banner advertisements and most animated icons are created.

JPEG

works well for photographs and continuous tone images, but generally have bigger file sizes, so take longer to transfer.

Editing images

When you edit your images for the web page, make sure that you use a good image editor that can support several different image file formats; products such as PhotoShop (*www.adobe.com*) and PaintShopPro (*www.shareware.com*) are popular for site designers.

Reducing file size

Speed up your web site by cutting down the size of each image to remove wasted space. A couple of techniques include:

- Reduce the number of colours used in an image – often without noticably reducing the quality of the image, but drastically reducing the size of the image file.
- Set the resolution (or use the software's re-scan feature) of the image to 72dpi – the resolution of most monitors. Any higher than this is generally wasted on displayed images and simply increases the size of the image file.
- Save your image files in an interlaced GIF format. Although not all browsers support this, it has the effect of building up the image gradually on the page rather than line by line, so giving the impression of greater speed.

Safe colour palette

When designing a web page, it's tempting to use the full range of colours from the palette. This gives free reign to your creative spirit when designing logos, navigation buttons and so on. However, there is one problem: not every user will have the same computer that you are using; not all web browsers or computers can display the same wide range of colours.

To get around this problem, there is a well-known palette of 'safe' colours that you can be sure will be displayed the same way on any type of browser and computer (for example, if a user is running an old version of Netscape Navigator on a Macintosh they will use a different base palette to your PC running the latest version of Microsoft IE).

Stick to the internet-safe palette colours, or your site will look a mess. A non-safe colour will be dithered (speckly and made up of two different colours) when displayed on a system that does not have the exact colour match.

Most web page design programs provide this palette of safe colours as standard, but if you are creating the pages manually, the palette is easy to create: the safe colours have RGB (red, green, blue) values that are multiples of 51 (or 33 in hexadecimal code that's used to specify colours in HTML). For example, values of 51, 102, 153, 204, 255 are safe.

Transparent Colours

One neat technique that is used in just about every web site is to define a transparent colour within an image. This trick only works with GIF images and sets one colour (it can be any colour) to appear transparent when displayed; this provides a good way of displaying highly formatted text. For example, if you want to add your company logo, create the GIF image file, set the background colour to transparent and place the logo on your web page. Most image editors and web page design tools include a feature to set one colour to appear transparent.

Animated graphics

One of the best ways of getting attention is to add movement to your images. This is particularly useful on a banner advert (studies show greatly improved response rates for animated banner ads – see Chapter 9). However, you can add animation to any image to create moving buttons, logos or other features. The only rule is keep it simple and limit your urge to become the next Walt Disney. More than one animation on a page looks silly!

To create animated images you use a version of the GIF image file format; the format is made up of several still images that are then displayed in order over a time, giving the effect of animation. There are plenty of image tools that will help you create these animated GIF images including tools from Sausage Software *(www.sausage.com)*; many other animation tools are shareware and available from *www.shareware.com.*

The user does not have to download any special applet (as they would with a Shockwave or other Java-based animation technique), but this form of animation is far more limited than the more complex systems such as Shockwave *(www.shockwave.com)*.

Image Maps

A feature of HTML lets you add a hypertext link to any image; this works well for buttons or icons that will take the user to another page when selected. A similar technique lets you add define areas on an image that each have a different hyperlink. For example, if your clothing store site displays one image of a well-dressed man, there could be one area defined to cover his jacket, another over his trousers, another over his shoes, his tie and so on. Each area is invisible to the viewer but is has a different hypertext link to a different page.

There are several ways of producing this effect, the usual is to use a client-side image map. This uses a set of HTML commands to define the coordinates of each area of the image; you should be able to use your web page design tool to create image maps. This technique does not work on very early versions of the Netscape web browser, but for most sites this is a convenient and effective way of providing a neat navigation tool.

Tricks with colour
There are plenty of tricks that you can use to add extra touches to your web site. These often use a combination of colour and programming to make an element stand out or to attract the user's attention.

Highlighting an element
One of the popular new web page design tricks is to change the colour of text or an image as a user moves their pointer over the element. For example, if you have a contents panel with five text items describing different parts of your web site, you can add a small script to change the text colour as the user moves his mouse pointer over the text.

This trick is normally carried out using a little Javascript program inserted into your main web page HTML file (visit *www.freescripts.com* for different examples).

Design features in a web page
Web pages are created using HTML codes that describe text, colour, images, and links to other pages. HTML (hypertext markup language) is a simple language and is not very suitable for describing complex page designs.

For example, if you want a web page to have a white background and display a headline in bold and the body text in italic, then HTML can do this very easily (using the <B> command for bold and <I> for italic).

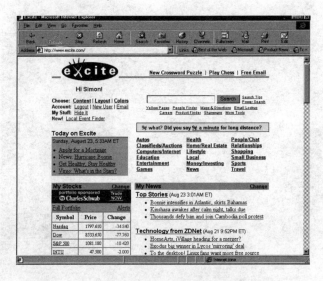

If you want to position images in a particular area of the page or if you want a page with several columns of text, you will need to use some of the more advanced HTML commands. Perhaps the most useful is the 'table' command. This was originally included to allow nicely formatted tables (a price list or similar) to be displayed. However, it is one of the keys to providing better layout control over your web page: each cell in the table can contain anything, not just a simple number. You can insert an image, text, link or other media into a cell. By creating a table with multiple columns and rows, you can divide your page into a grid that gives you more control when positioning media.

In the next pages, I cover some of the ways of extending HTML to provide better layout, neat effects, forms, search engines and so on.

NOTE: One of the problems of pushing HTML to its limits or using these extended features is that they are not supported by every type of web browser. To get around this problem, you should either design to the lowest common denominator or use a script to detect the capabilities of the visitor's web browser and adjust accordingly.

Hypertext Links

An important feature of HTML is that it can include links which allow a user to jump from one web page to another related page simply by clicking on the word or image. These hypertext links are entered using standard HTML codes; you can define any text or image to act as a link – the active word will be displayed underlined and (generally) in blue – although this colour can be changed. The user's mouse pointer changes from an arrow to a hand when it passes over a link.

You can use hypertext links to provide quick links to background information, to further details, an order form or another section of your web site. If you have a large, high-resolution image of your product, you could include a small thumbnail image on your main page and a link the thumbnail to the larger image. This way, the user is not forced to wait for the larger image to download before viewing the page and can select if he wants to see the high-resolution image.

NOTE: one of the most annoying features of a site is missing, incorrect or broken links. It shows that the site has been poorly tested or is not kept up to date. Use web design software that can test the links – such as Adobe's PageMill, Microsoft FrontPage, NetObjects or HotDog or use a special link-check tool such as LinkBot *(www.linkbot.com)*. If you include links to other external sites that are out of your control, provide a feedback page or email address to allow visitors to report broken links – however, it's better to run a check on a regular basis.

Page Layout

The HTML language is very limiting for designers who want to position elements in an exact place on the page. Unlike a DTP program that allows you to place text anywhere on the page, HTML tags only allow you to align text or an image to either the left or right margin or cen-tred. So how do you create a complex, good-looking web page with multiple columns? The answer is to use either two HTML features that allow you to create tables and frames within a web page.

Simple Tables

The simplest method is to create a table that covers the main part of your page. The table is made up rows and columns; each cell of the table can contain material. For example, if you want to have an image in the bottom right-hand corner of your page, insert the image into this cell.

Within each cell, standard HTML formatting commands work as normal, so your image (or text) can be aligned to the left, right or central margins of the cell. Each cell can have different formatting and even a different background colour. When designing with tables, it's useful to set the table border to a width of one so that you can see the size of the table. When you publish your page, set the border to zero and your table's grid lines disap-pear.

Although tables are a little cumbersome to set up and manipulate, they are simple and almost every browser will support tables. This is a great plus point – compared to frames that are only supported by the newer range of browsers. The only caveat to this is that some older web browsers, notably Netscape Navigator 2, do not correctly reproduce cell background colours.

NOTE: Check the *www.browserwatch.com* site and *www.webdeveloper.com* for up-to-date details about the different browser technologies and the fea-tures that each supports.

Flexible Frames

The second method of designing the layout of your page is to use frames. This is a newer, more complex feature of HTML that is only supported in the newer versions of Navigator and Microsoft IE, but it is attractive enough to find its way on to many sites.

Frames allow a web page to be split into different, independent regions. One main web page defines the frame sizes, positions and attributes and loads the content for each frame from separate files.

This means that you can have a constant 'frame' with a constant index bar, logo and navigation panel whilst the changing content is displayed in the central section of the page.

Frames are very powerful and, with good design, can make a complex site clean and easy to navigate. All good web design tools support frame-based page design. However, it is well worth including a <noframes> tag that includes code used to display a simpler page if a visitor's web browser is not capable of supporting frames.

Forms in HTML

When creating a web site, it's important to involve the visitor whenever possible. This means asking them to enter information that can then be processed by the web server. In a passive web site, the visitor simply views web pages, reads the information and follows hyperlinks. In an active web site, they enters a search term and see results or fill in an order form or enter a discussion group.

Any time you want to ask a visitor to enter information, you are using form; HTML form codes allow a web designer to add text entry boxes, list boxes, check box and radio buttons and various other feedback elements.

Once you have designed the form elements on your web page, the real work can start. A button, text box or list will allow the visitor to type in text or select an option but that's all. There's no processing function provided by HTML or form codes. The form merely collects the information from the visitor and passes it to a separate program that can then act on this information to produce a result. This separate program is normally created using the Perl or C programming language, but it could be a database system or any other type of proprietary back-end linked to your web server.

The two functions of form commands are to display fields and buttons on the user's web browser and then to tell the web browser what to do with the information when the designated 'go' button is clicked. As I have just mentioned, the usual route is to pass the information from the form fields to a separate program. The method of passing this information is called CGI and the separate program is therefore called a CGI script – even if it is written in the Perl or C programming language.

The visual element of the form commands describe many different styles of input field including:

- text box
- radio button
- checkbox
- password text box that displays an asterisk when any character is pressed
- active image that returns the coordinates of the visitor's mouse pointer and is used in image maps
- listbox that allows a user to select an option from a list
- listbox that allows a user to select and send a file
- button that submits the form's data to the processing program
- button that will cancel and clear the form.

For example, many sites now provide a newsletter or bulletin that is delivered by email. The site normally makes it easy for any visitor to sign up as a subscriber and receive the bulletin using just two form elements: a text box into which the visitor enters their email address and a submit button that sends the email address to the mailing list program.

Behind this simple form, the site developers will have had to create a program that processes the email address, displays a 'thank you for subscribing' page and adds the visitor's email address to the main mailing list.

Another common example is a feedback form. Although the visual form looks more complex – with fields for the user's name, address, comments and so on, the program behind the scenes is much simpler and normally just combines the replies from each field into one email message that is then forwarded to the web site administrator.

Online shopping systems that allow a visitor to select items from display and add them to a virtual shopping basket are far more complex. These use forms to display lists of products, then ask the visitor to enter the quantity for the order and, finally, ask for the visitor's payment details. The information from each form is managed by a large quite complex program that has a database of product information, price per product and quantity in stock. The software records the customer's details with the product selection and stores this in another database together with delivery details, etc. All this occurs on the computer that is hosting the web server – either in-house or, more likely, at the internet service provider.

Style Sheets

Style sheets are a new and convenient way of simplifying text formatting within a web page. Normally called cascading style sheets, CSS, these work in a similar way to the style settings in a word processor. They cover the font, size, colour, position, margins and so on. Any text can be given a pre-defined style rather than have to re-enter the individual settings.

The drawback of style sheets is that, as a new feature, they are currently only supported by the Microsoft IE 3 and Netscape Navigator 4 web browsers – and even these two versions are not quite compatible. If you do use style sheets, make quite sure that your pages are tested with older browser technology and still look just as good.

One way of creating style sheets is to use a linked style sheet file. This separate file contains definitions of all the styles used across the entire web site. It allows different designers to coordinate their efforts and ensure that the results are cohesive. The alternative is to use an embedded style sheet; for this, the style definition is included as part of a standard web page HTML file and so the styles are only available to this one page.

Enhancing the browser

So far, all the features that I have described allow a web designer to use standard HTML codes which are then interpreted by the visitor's web browser. Since the range of functions provided by HTML is limiting, especially when it comes to multimedia support, there has to be another system available.

The way of providing extra sophisticated functionality on a web page is to use a program that runs within the user's own web browser (not on the main computer where the site is stored). These tiny programs are normally called applets or, if they work to enhance the web browser, a plug-in. Two main programming systems that have attracted a lot of attention over the past few years are Java and ActiveX, developed by Sun Microsystems and Microsoft respectively.

These two systems allow a programmer to create an applet that will be downloaded automatically when a visitor enters the web site. The applet will then run on the visitor's own computer and provide some neat feature, such as displaying current stock quotes or processing live video, sound or animation.

Creating a Java or ActiveX program is not easy and is best left to a professional programmer. It is also beginning to cause a few problems; the main being do you really want an unknown program from an unknown web site to be automatically run on your computer? Answer, no. Solution, provide authentication for each applet.

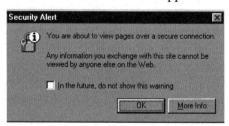

Authentication offers a way of proving to a visitor that you are who you claim to be and that your software is trustworthy. A web browser will normally warn the user that it is about to start automatically downloading an applet and will ask the user if they want to see the certificate of authentication for this company and applet. It's a sort of passport for applets that you can check.

If you include applets on your site to provide a neat function, remember that plenty of users will stop the download, especially if you do not provide an authentication certificate (see sites such as *www.verisign.com* for details on authentication). The other disadvantage of applets is that they will only work with compatible web browsers – Java is the most popular system of the two and works on the newer versions of Netscape Navigator and Microsoft IE (look at the *www.browserwatch.com* site for details on compatibility).

Scripting languages

In the previous section, I described programming systems that allow a designer to create a stand-alone program or applet that runs on the user's computer within the web browser. There is another system of extending HTML and so extending the functions provided by the user's web browser ~ by using a scripting language.

Scripts are a series of commands that are included as part of a standard web page. The web browser runs each script command that form the tiny program. The functionality is limited compared to an applet, but it's a great way of adding neat features to your web site with little programming experience.

There are two main scripting systems: JavaScript and VBScript developed by Netscape and Microsoft respectively. Although it has a similar name, JavaScript bears little relation to the Java programming language used to create an applet. However, JavaScript and Java fit together very well to provide a complete way of enhancing your web site: JavaScript allows a designer to control the way a web browser works, but cannot draw graphics or carry out networking functions. Java, on the other hand, can draw graphics and support complex networking functions but cannot directly control the functions of the browser.

Of the two systems, JavaScript is in far greater use than VBScript, although both are similar in concept and functionality. As with the other features described here, JavaScript will only work on Netscape Navigator 3 or Microsoft IE 3 web browsers (Navigator version 2 supported some of the commands). To use VBScript, you will need to run Microsoft IE 3.

A scripting language such as JavaScript is great for neat features that add sparkle to your web site. One of the most popular current tricks is to change the colour of a menu item or icon as the user passes their mouse pointer over. This is normally carried out with a simple JavaScript program, just a few lines long included at the start of the web page HTML file. Other ways of using JavaScript include displaying a dialog box to ask the user to enter information, carrying out mathematical functions and processing time and date information.

The web is full of libraries with free sample JavaScript scripts that you can use in your own site; two include *www.webdeveloper.com* and *www.freecode.com*.

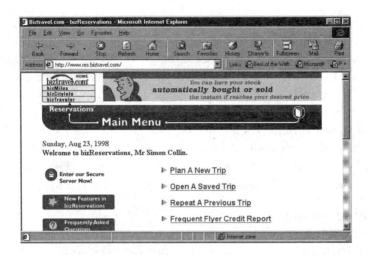

NOTE: if your web site uses JavaScript, use a script on the homepage to check if the visitor's web browser supports JavaScript and if not, display a simpler page designed for older browsers.

Multimedia presentations

An alternative to creating your own programs using Java or ActiveX is to use an authoring system designed specifically for a job. There are several systems available that allow designers (rather than programmers) to create stunning multimedia effects that can be displayed on a web browser.

The user still has to download a special control applet to allow his browser to support the system, but once they have this installed, the user can view any of your multimedia creations. You do not need to install any special software on the web server, simply store the multimedia presentation file on the server and include a link to the software company to allow visitors to download the standard (free) control applet.

One of the most popular multimedia authoring systems for the web is called Shockwave. This system, developed by Macromedia *(www.macromedia.com)* lets you add multimedia functions to your Web pages. Using Shockwave you can add animation, presentations, movement and audio using the Shockwave developer's kit.

Three-dimensional worlds

One of the most visually impressive functions available on the web allows you to create real-time three-dimensional images. As the user moves around the web site, they see new 3D scenes. This works well for some applications, such as games, but is not always ideal for business sites.

The technique to create these virtual worlds is to design a landscape using an authoring system called VRML (virtual reality modeling language). You will also need special 3D scene creation software, such as 3D Builder from Virtus Corporation *(www.virtus.com)* or VRCreator from Vream *(www.vream.com)*, to develop scenes that can then be viewed using any compatible browser.

To allow the standard Microsoft or Netscape web browsers to view a VRML scene, the user has to download a special control applet to allow the browser to support the new data format. When you visit a web site that uses VRML, you'll be prompted if you want to download a plug-in. For more information on this technology, and sources of the plug-ins, see the home site at *www.vrml.com* or *visit www.sgi*.com to see more information from the developers, Silicon Graphics.

Paper publishing online

If your business publishes a magazine, newspaper, journal or books, then you are probably rather irritated that you have to duplicate the design effort to use the clumsy HTML formatting language for online versions of your publications.

There are several techniques that allow you to publish complex, highly-formatted documents on to the web – without losing any fonts, images or layout. These systems encapsulate the original design (perhaps created with Quark xPress or Corel Ventura DTP software) and convert it into a new document format. You can now store this document on your web site and any visitor with a compatible web browser will see the original document, complete with fonts and formatting.

There are a few conditions to this system. First, the user needs to download a special control applet for their web browser (although this is not complicated) and second, the content still appears as a static page rather than allowing you to create it on-the-fly as you might with the results from a database. These publishing techniques do provide a way to provide high-quality documents online, but they are still simply static versions of the original paper media – although there are developments to change this.

The most popular system is Adobe's Acrobat software system *(www.adobe.com)* that allows you to publish the same formatted document as a searchable document on CD-ROM, the web or to paper. Other products include Corel Barista *(www.corel.com)*.

External scripts and programs

So far in this chapter, I have covered the different ways of presenting information on a web page. You can use standard HTML formatting codes to set out text and include images and links. To enhance the page, you can use applets or scripts to work with the user's web browser. However, all these features are, generally, centred on the user.

One of the key elements to any large or sophisticated web site is the programs that run on the web server itself (and not, as with an applet, on the user's computer). Sites that provides a search facility, online ordering, a discussion group or any other sophisticated, interactive feature carry out these functions using external programs which run on the web server computer.

Many of the applications I have described within this book are implemented using a program running on a server. For example, if you want to set up a large, automated mailing list management system, you would install a majordomo or list-server program on the web server. If you want to add a search feature or database link, this would normally be via a custom-written program. Similarly, if you include a form (see earlier, this chapter) on your web page, you need a program to process the information entered into the form.

Programs that run on a web server can be written in a wide range of programming languages. One of the most popular is called Perl, others include C, Visual Basic, and proprietary database programming languages. Once you have written your program, you store the program file on the web server in much the same way that you store your web page files. Information is passed between the web page (for example, the form that asks for a search term) and the program using a system called CGI (common gateway interface). As a result, programs are sometimes referred to as CGI scripts.

If you plan to add a feature, such as a shopping cart or search engine, you can install a commercial product or write the program yourself. Better still, look at the libraries of free software programs – plenty of programmers still work to the freeware model that formed the internet – and adapt these to your own requirements. For example, *www.freecode.com* and *www.freescript.com* both list hundreds of different programs covering a whole range of topics.

Customise with Cookies

Providing visitors with customised web pages is a great advantage and not too difficult to achieve using the 'cookies' feature. Cookies are markers stored in a configuration file on the user's computer; any site can create their own marker in this file using simple JavaScript commands. The marker could include the user's registered name, when they last visited the site or their preference for display language (these would be pulled from a feedback form and then saved within the marker.

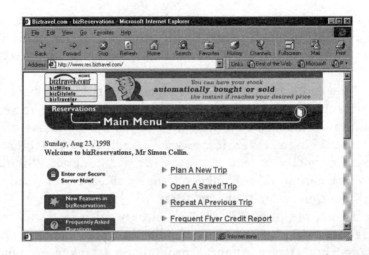

Cookies are slightly contentious because the web site is writing information into the user's computer – normally without the user realising this is happening. However, user's can switch off the cookie feature within their web browser to protect themselves.

A nice way of using cookies is to include a record of the last order shipped to a visitor. For example, if you sell wine, your web site could automatically greet the visitor with 'Hello Simon, it's been three weeks since your last visit. You bought Claret and might like to see our new range of wines from Bordeaux'. The information on the user's name, date and last purchase are stored in the cookie file and the rest is calculated by a background program.

Chat and discussion

Mention chat to a savvy internet user, and they immediately think of Internet Relay Chat (IRC) that has become rather infamous as a way of arguing or even dating over the net. IRC uses a rather primitive user interface and is hardly friendly. In Chapter 6 I explain ways of adding a discussion group or live chat to your web site to involve the visitors.

The two main server technologies behind the change in chat from command-line to web browser are the Palace Commercial Server and the paraCHAT server from Paralogic. paraCHAT is written in Java and requires the clients to download and use a Java plug-in. Once the server is set up, the manager can define the users allowed to access the chat sessions. Instead of a real-time chat session, other products support discussion forums, such as Proxicom Forum that allows newsgroup-style discussion groups via a web browser. The final trend is to support 'rooms' in which users can chat about different subjects; this model is supported by the ichat server from Itropolis.

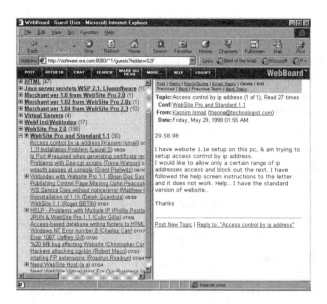

Not surprisingly, both Netscape and Microsoft have launched products that allow users to participate in chat or discussion forums from their web browser. Each uses a different method and requires different plug-ins on the browser. In addition to the usual moderator features, these also support SSL to ensure that your private company discussions remain private.

Conferencing and chat servers

NAME	URL
ChatWare	www.eware.com
Commercial Internet System (Microsoft)	www.microsoft.com
Community System (Netscape)	home.netscape.com
ichat (Itropolis)	www.ichat.com
The Palace Commercial Server	www.thepalace.com
paraCHAT (Paralogic)	parachat.webpage.com
Proxicom Forum	www.proxicom.com

Web broadcasts

The latest design-led web sites attempt to turn the web into a multimedia experience with animation, sound, video clips and so on. This does not always work, mainly due to the limitations of the technology at the user's end. A better alternative is to use snippets of multimedia to enhance a site or to provide a unique feature, such as a live broadcast or interview. For example, if your company produces audio-books, you can include a section of audio on your site. If you have just completed a spectacular new building, include a short video tour of the building. The key, as with all specialist technologies, is to ensure that the majority of your visitors whose browsers do not support web-based multimedia still get some information.

One of the most popular features is live audio transmission over the web. Just visit commercial radio station *www.virgin.co.uk* and you'll hear the same radio broadcast – via your browser. The process of delivering the multimedia material is more complex than you might first imagine.

To provide a smooth, clear, unbroken video or radio clip, the web server needs to send a continuous stream of data over the Internet to the user's web browser. Unfortunately, the web was never designed for long, continuous streams of data so new standards have been developed. These work at both ends: the web server uses special software to broadcast the multimedia and the web browser uses a special plug-in applet to decode the multimedia.

There are many different standards used to deliver sound and video over the Internet including Progressive Network's RealAudio, Microsoft's NetShow server (that supports both audio and video) and Netscape's MediaServer. Each of these streaming data technologies allow the user or publisher to limit the delivery of data to a maximum data rate. There are several standard formats used including Microsoft's multimedia delivery format, ASF (active streaming format) and other standards developed by Macromedia, VDOnet, Vivo, and VXtreme.

If you plan to broadcast multimedia presentations, you should talk to your internet service provider: your requirements will probably exceed their basic business throughput (the amount of data you are allowed to send per day).

Multimedia servers

NAME	AUDIO	VIDEO	URL
Media Server (Netscape)	yes	no	home.netscape.com
NetShow (Microsoft)	yes	yes	www.microsoft.com
RealMedia (Progressive Networks)	yes	yes	www.realaudio.com
StreamWorks (Xing)	yes	yes	www.xingtech.com
VDOLive (VDOnet)	yes	yes	www.vdo.com
WebTheater (VXtreme)	yes	yes	www.vxtreme.com

Storing your Web pages on the Internet

When you design and create the web pages that make up your site, the files are normally stored on your computer's hard disk. (If you have your own in-house intranet, you will probably store the files on the main server.) To allow users to see your web pages, you will need to publish them on to the web. This is actually a very simple process and involves copying all the files that make up the site on to the server that is hosting your web site.

For example, if you are using an ISP to host your web site (most companies opt for this to start with, since it provides a low-cost and low-risk entry point) then you will need to transfer the files from your hard disk to the storage area on the ISP's server computer. To copy files to another computer you need to use a special software utility that manages FTP (file transfer protocol); your ISP will provide complete instructions that explain how to connect and log on to their server and copy your files – each ISP has different procedures.

To make life rather easier, many of the better web page design programs (such as FrontPage, PageMill and HotDog) include all the features that you need to publish your web site. With these programs, all you need to do is to configure the software to tell it the name of the ISP's server computer (its domain name) and your access password. Once you have finished designing the pages, click on the publish button and the software does the rest.

Once you have uploaded your Web page files, anyone can view them by entering your domain name URL into their browser - for example 'www.MyCompany.co.uk' or by referencing an individual page, for example 'www.MyCompany.co.uk/order-form.html'

Conclusions

New tools have ensured that the process of creating a web site is very easy – however, this is no guarantee of good design or functionality. To create a useful, friendly and successful web site will take the individual efforts of marketing, design, programming and content supply. By making web design easier, the Internet has been deluged with poorly-designed over-fussy sites that offer nothing new to the visitor.

Spending a little time working through what you can offer and analysing the target audience and their requirements will provide you with an immediate list of features that should be included on your site. In this chapter I outlined the different features you can provide on your web site and explained how they work and are installed (use and benefit are covered in individual chapters through the rest of the book). By following some of the ideas for design, colour, fonts and images, you will be at a great advantage over the slower, poorly-designed sites that occupy most of the web.

CHAPTER 4
Promoting your site

A great web site not only looks good, but is also carefully promoted so that users know that it exists and where to find it. For an effective web site promotion campaign, you need to plan the publicity in parallel with the design of the site. If you wait until the site is up and running, you are too late.

After spending time and effort planning and designing your web site you need to make sure that it gets all the publicity it deserves. There are many thousands of new web sites launched every day so you need to make sure that, against this competition, your site gets noticed.

There are dozens of different ways to promote your site and your planning must include both traditional and new online channels. Quite apart from informing potential visitors, customers and press, you will also have to inform the online search databases – the key to a high profile on the web. This chapter covers the different techniques of site promotion and provides tips on how best to index your site with the main search engines.

Announcing your web site

Your aim is to ensure that the greatest number of visitors enter your site; the method is to promote your web site to the widest audience. You need to use a whole range of techniques – from basic marketing to simple programming. The following steps will provide good coverage and make sure that your web site gets off to a great start. If you are re-launching or re-designing your site, you should use the same basic steps. As you can see from this list, there is a lot of work to do to prepare the ground before you announce the site to the press and public.

- prepare your web pages by including indexing information
- submit your site to the main search engines
- submit your site to *online review* and *what's new* sites
- find trade organizations and ask if they will include a link to you from their site
- find related web sites and ask for reciprocal links
- search for BusinessLink and local government sponsored business sites and ask for reciprocal links
- make sure that the new site address is on company advertising and stationery

- modify any email or newsgroup signatures to show your new web address
- research banner advertising to increase exposure
- send out a press release to newspapers, magazines, agencies, online newsletters
- inform key customers and distributors
- monitor relevant newsgroups and post minimal but quality information
- monitor relevant mailing lists and post minimal but quality information
- consider using targeted email lists for direct publicity to increase visitors

Search engines: the key to being found

Perhaps the most important step is to ensure that your web site is correctly registered with the main web search engines. These search engines (Yahoo!, AltaVista, Excite!, InfoSeek and so on) are rather like a giant indexed telephone directory to all the web sites on the Internet. A user enters search key words and the search engine lists all the sites that match the criteria. Some sites, notably Yahoo!, also organise the entries under headings – rather like a Yellow Pages. If you are looking for direct-mail companies, you would select the Companies/Marketing/Direct-mail section for a complete list.

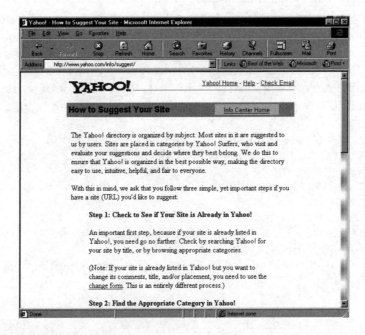

Your first job is to make sure that your web site is correctly listed and indexed. When the web was starting out, there were only a few million pages stored and so the search engines could keep up to date with new pages and sites by sending out automated robots (called spiders) that searched the web for new or changed pages that could be added to their index. Once you created a new web site you could be pretty sure that it would be automatically listed and indexed. This is no longer the case!

There are thousands of new web sites created every day and the search engines simply cannot keep up with the job of scanning and indexing all the new material. To solve the problem, all the major engines allow you to register your site; once you have told the search engine that your new site exists and provided basic description and information about your site, the search engine will send out a robot spider that will check through all the pages of your site and add each as a new entry in the index.

There are two ways of registering your web site with a search engine: you can visit the search engine and manually fill out an electronic registration form or you can use an automated program to do this work for you across all the search engines. Visiting each search engine yourself takes time, but lets you enter exactly the information you want to appear on the search index. If you use an automated program to do the work, it will ask you once for short and long descriptions of your site and submit these to the search engines. You cannot then tailor the information to each index, but it does save a lot of time!

The good news about automated registration programs is that they will normally provide a free service in which your site's details are sent to a dozen of the top search engines. If you want the registration program to send the information to every search engine on the Internet, you will have to pay for this. For most sites, it is only worth registering with the top 25 search engines. There are over 300 search engines available, but the majority of users will stick to a couple of favourites. See later in this chapter for a list of major search engines and submissions services.

Before you register your web site with any search engine, you must make sure that each page making up the site has extra information that is used to help the search engine to correctly index the site.

Prepare your web pages for indexing
To ensure that your web site is correctly indexed, web search engines now look in part to the page designers to provide key information about the contents of the site. This means that you need to write a short description and provide key words for each page on your site. If you do not do this, the search engines will simply use the first few sentences of text in each page.

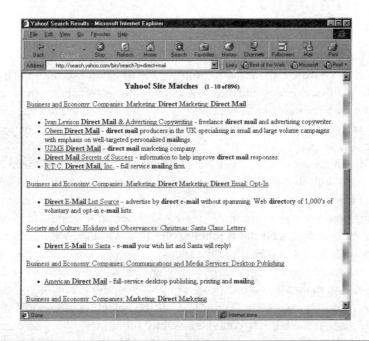

PREPARE YOUR PAGES HOWEVER YOU REGISTER
You should make sure that each page within your web site includes the indexing information listed in the three steps to provide a page title, key-words and description. Make sure that the information is relevant to the page and not just copied between pages. Even if you use an automatic sub-mission service, you will still need to include this information.

1. Page title

Make sure that each page on your site has a clear, concise title. There's no need to include your company name, but you should ensure that the title describes the contents of the page. For example, if you are a publisher of reference books, the page about your law dictionary should have a title 'Dictionary of Law – the definitive reference for students' or similar. Do not give all your web pages a generic title such as 'Big Reference Publisher Inc. web site'.

The page title appears in three important places: first, it is displayed at the top of the user's browser window, second it is used as the title for a bookmark index if a user has cre-ated a bookmark to your page. Third, and most importantly, it is used as the title for your index by the search engine.

To create a page title, use your web page design software to enter the title for each page. If your page design software does not let you enter the page title (almost all do), you can use the <TITLE>..</TITLE> HTML code within the HTML file for the page. This line should be near the top of the code for your page, within the <HEADER>...</HEADER> tags. For example:

<TITLE> Dictionary of Law - the definitive reference for students</TITLE>

2. Enter the keywords

You can provide a list of keywords to help the search engine. These key words (between 50 and 100 words) are the words that someone would enter at the search engine to find your site. These words are added within a special type of HTML code, called a META tag, that is not visible with a web browser but which is used by the search engines to index your site. You will normally have to add to your web page by using a code editor – most page design products allow you to enter HTML code directly or you can use a text editor to edit the final HTML file.

The keywords can contain terms or phrases, separated by a comma, but you should not repeat a word more than three times. Use the following META tag to list the code for your web page – the line should be near the top of the page, within the <HEADER>...</HEADER> section and in the following format:

<META NAME="KEYWORDS" CONTENT="dictionary, law, legal, reference book, law student">

3. Describe your page

The final preparatory step is to create a description for your page. This should be a concise description that is between 200-250 characters long. The simplest way to do this is to choose the most important dozen keywords from step two and use these to create a readable description. However, keep the descriptive sentences short and terse and remove any padding or non-vital words.

This description will be displayed by the search engine under the page title in response to a search from a user. Most search engines will only display the first 150-200 characters of a description. If you do not include this description in each page, the search engine will use the first lines of text displayed on your page.

It is worth noting that some search engines, most notably Yahoo!, use real editors to trim down and read these page descriptions, so make sure that they meet the submission requirements. Lastly, if your page matches a search then the description is shown just beneath your web page title, so there is no need to include the words or sentence used for your page title in step 1.

The page description is added within another META tag and stored near the top of the web page between the <HEADER>...</HEADER> tags. As with step 2, above, the META tag description is not visible with a web browser but that is used by the search engines to help index your site. You will normally have to add to your web page by using a code editor - most page design products allow you to enter HTML code directly or you can use a text editor to edit the final HTML file. The code should look like:

<META NAME="DESCRIPTION" CONTENT="Dictionary that provides up to date coverage of law. Find clear definitions to legal terms. Understand complex law reports. Recommended by major exam boards">

Submit your site to search engines

Once you have prepared each page in your web site with a title and the two different META tags, you are ready to submit the pages to the search engines. As mentioned earlier, you can do this manually be visiting each of the major search engines and manually completing a submission form or you can use a commercial service that will automatically submit this information to a range of sites. If you are in a hurry, use one of the automatic submission services such as www.submit-it.com, *www.exploit.com, www.did-it.com* or *www.all4one.com*. However, since each search engine has slightly different registration requirements you will get a better fit if you have the time to visit each manually.

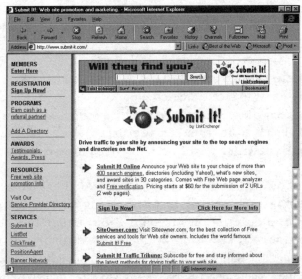

The submission requirements for each search engine is different and tend to change. The most important of the lot is a good submission to Yahoo!. Visit their submission instruction page (*www.yahoo.com/docs/info*) to make sure that you follow the instructions carefully. You can keep up to date with current information about submission methods by looking at the invaluable www.searchenginewatch.com web site.

Important Search Engines

Whether you decide to add your new web site to each search engine manually or to use a commercial system that will add the new domain automatically, you should make sure that the site is registered with the following important sites:

www.altavista.digital.com
www.excite.com
www.hotbot.com
www.infoseek.com
www.lycos.com
www.yahoo.com
www.webcrawler.com

Online review and 'what's new' listings

To help users keep in touch with the best of the new sites, there are dozens of very popular "what's new" sites. These listings sometimes use a review panel to review new sites or list any new site submitted or request payment for a listing. Users visit the lists to see what's new and exciting on the web. In general, this type of listing is second only to the main search engines for popularity – so it is very worth while submitting your site to as many of these directories as possible.

The directories are run by a range of organizations, from internet magazines – these tend to display fewer sites that have been reviewed – or large search engines or companies or hobbyists. With the exception of the major 'new' directory sites (listed below), the other directories tend to come and go. Turn the tables and use a search engine to find the latest sites that contain a "what's new" section.

www.yahoo.com/picks
www.netscape.com
www.internet-magazine.com/sites
www.infoseek.com
or look at the very useful CyberOnline site that lists more than 600 award and 'what's new' sites: *www.resoluteinc.com/cyberonline/600awards.htm*

When you submit your site to a non-paying directory, you will be asked for similar information that is required when listing your site on a search engine. The best tactic is to make sure that your submission is readable is:

1. visit the registration page of each what's new site
2. bookmark the page (press Ctrl-B within your web browser)
3. print out the page with its submission form
4. decide off-line how to fill in the key words and descriptions
5. type all the details into a word processor
6. connect to the web, find the site with bookmark, cut-and-paste your pre-written answers.

Ask for reciprocal links

One of the best ways of reaching a niche market is to ask another web site with a similar or related profile if they will include a link to your web site – make it a reciprocal deal and offer to include a link back to their site. With the exception of direct competitors, most other related sites should be happy to include a reciprocal link; they, too, are trying to promote their site.

Use the main search engines to help find all your sites and organizations (see Chapter 11 for more details on researching on the Internet). Once you have a list, visit the sites and see if the site contains links to other related sites. Send an email message to the contact or to the webmaster to ask for a link.

Trade organizations

Almost every industry has at least one related trade organization and they are likely to have a web site. Ask if they will include a reciprocal link to your web site within their pages. They might have a list of member-companies or related links that could prove to be a good source of visitors to your site. The organization will be trying to promote its own site to its members and might be happy to include a link.

Related businesses

Your business must have dozens of close ties to other companies; your main distributors, customers or partners might have web sites. Ask if they will include a reciprocal link.

For example, if you supply teaching materials, visit the various exam board sites to see if they have lists of related links. Search for teacher forums sites that provide lists of online resources. Some educational bookshops or distributors would also have lists of related sites.

Similar sites
A different method of attack is to find the sites that you think might attract similar visitors and mail the webmaster with a request to add a reciprocal link. If you spend a lot of time at a few key sites, the chances are that they important to your company or industry and might accept a reciprocal link.

Analyze log files
One way of finding which other sites appeal to your visitors is to view the detail from your site's access log. Some logging systems can try and capture the name of previous web sites that person visited before entering your sites. (See Chapter 5 for more details.) You can also use the access logs to see the popular domain types from which users are visiting; this might give you a clue to the countries to which you appeal.

For example, if you supply a service to mend enamel baths, you might find visitors are trying to find you by visiting plumbers or bathroom supply stores. Some of these sites might be happy to add a link to your site to give their visitors the impression of adding information and providing a community spirit. You might find that half your visitors first visit the site of a major distributor. In which case, why not ask them to put a direct link in place?. For details on producing this type of script, see Chapter 3.

BusinessLink and local government sites
Many local government-sponsored schemes, such as BusinessLink, have comprehensive web sites with general business information, tips and support. Many of the sites include directories of companies in the area listed by role or product. These sites provide a good resource if you are looking for a local company to provide a service, so turn the tables and make sure that your site is listed as supplier.

Include your web address - everywhere
You have gone to considerable effort to set up your web site, now make sure that the domain name is included on all your company material. Make sure that the domain name is on your business cards, letterhead and other company stationery.

When you create advertisements, include your domain name and an email contact on each advert. Similarly, make sure that new catalogues, price lists and flyers all have your web site address. Conventions usually print a catalogue of exhibitors and are often used as a reference by the visitors – make sure that your catalogue entry includes your web site address.

Use signature files

Every electronic mail program and newsreader lets you create a signature file. This is automatically added to the end of any email message or posting to a newgroup and should provide your name, company, summary of services and domain name.

When you send email, the signature re-inforces the company brand. When you post a message to a newsgroup or discussion group or mailing list, the signature file is effectively your company's only advertising.

A signature can be almost any length. Some users like to include quotations or gags – avoid these! Stick to between five and eight lines and keep the information simple, factual and useful. Include your name, contact numbers, company name, company specialization or key product, such as 'makers of world-renowned white chocolates' and web site. Most mailing lists ask that signatures are limited to just four lines and should not have any slogans. Many email programs allow you to set up several different signatures, for just this purpose.

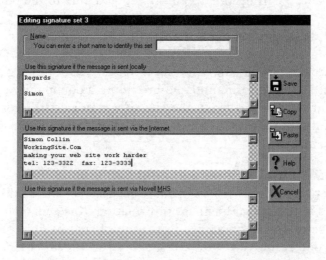

Make sure that you create similar signatures in your newsgroup reader so that the signature will be added to any message you post to a newsgroup. This way, you can participate in a newsgroup on an information-only basis – by replying to questions – but still provide a link to your company through your signature.

Banner advertising

A popular way of promoting your site is to use banner advertising, although its effectiveness has dropped to an average response rate of just one percent. Banner images are displayed on almost all commercial sites and link back to the adver-tiser's site. If you have a big budget, you can pay to place your banner ad in the vast, general search engine sites. For better targeting, you can consider advertising on niche sites. You do not even need to pay for banner advertising; the LinkExchange cooperative lets you exchange your banner image with other sites to increase visitors. Banner advertising is covered in detail in Chapter 9.

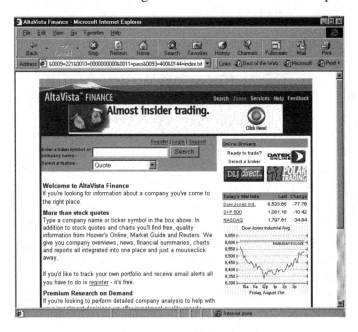

Press releases

Finally, after preparing the groundwork, you should now send a press release to your contacts announcing your new site. Send the release to your usual contact list, all trade journals for your industry and reporters at the main newspapers and magazines. You should also research the list of print magazines covering the Internet that list new site announcements – don't bother sending your news to magazines that specifically do not cover new sites.

Make sure that you include technical details of the way the site was implemented and how it benefits visitors. If your site provides an impressive technical resource or has clever programming, send the release to the more technical programming magazines – they often do profiles or how sites were created.

In Chapter 10, I cover the range of online agencies which can distribute your release by email to thousands of reporters, newspapers, magazines and news agencies. These companies provide a good way of ensuring that your release makes it to the greatest range of reporters.

Announce to customers

Make sure that you tell your existing customer base that your new web site is up and running. If you send out a newsletter, you will obviously include it in this. Otherwise, add a note to invoices or when sending out a requested catalogue. If there is real customer benefit – a free product, better access to information or online ordering – that you want to promote, consider sending a flyer to existing customers.

Use newsgroups and mailing lists

Once your web site is up and running, you can start to reinforce your company's profile and the site address by monitoring and posting information to newsgroups and mailing lists. Newsgroups are part of what is often called the Usenet. There are over 20,000 individual newsgroups which provide a forum covering almost every subject under the sun. There are many thousands more mailing lists covering similarly diverse niche subject areas.

Although there might be newsgroups and mailing lists that cover the same subjects, the two work in quite different ways. Anyone can join a newsgroup; each message (normally called an article) is posted to the newsgroup using a news-reader. The messages are arranged hierachically and grouped with replies to an article linked to the main article. This makes it easy for a user to follow a thread from question to answer. The information that makes up a newsgroup is stored on server computers for a period of time. Many of the larger search engines index the contents of a newsgroup, letting you search through every article.

Mailing lists work by email; to join a mailing list, you need to subscribe by sending a message to the list server (a piece of software). If a user wants to ask a question, she sends an email to the list server and the message is automatically distributed to every subscriber on the list. Mailing lists have rules and the managers will remove you if you post commercial messages or product adverts. Although you can search for a mailing list that serves your area of interest, you cannot search the actual contents of the messages, since these are not stored.

To promote your web site, you should monitor the newsgroups and mailing lists that cover your subject areas of interest. Use the specialist search engines, such as www.liszt.com and www.dejanews.com to find the newsgroups and mailing lists which match. Read the description of the mailing list and its code of practice to see if it welcomes new site announcements or restricts postings to academic discussion. Similarly, with newsgroups, look at past messages to see what is acceptable. You will need to read plenty of postings - many lists generate hundreds of messages every day – to check for messages that ask questions that you can answer.

Answer occasionally and with authority. The signature at the bottom of your email messages (for mailing lists) and newsreaders (for newsgroups) will be enough advertising in these sensitive channels. Do not use blatant product plugs and only suggest that other readers visit your site if there is a particular benefit. Don't write 'our new site has launched, please stop by'. Far better to say 'fellow woodworkers, we've published a range of free plans online at our new site'.

If you do promote a product or place a commercial message in a newsgroup or mailing list, then you will be flamed – you'll receive hate mail back from all the other members who do not appreciate the blatant advertising. See Chapter 7 for more details on this form of one-to-one publicity.

Direct email

An interesting route to reach a targeted range of potential customers is to use direct email. This method of marketing has been badly tarnished by heavy-handed marketeers who sent millions of unwanted email messages around the globe – clogging up user's mailboxes and the Internet itself.

However, there are now respectable companies offering lists of users you have indicated that they are willing to accept direct email messages about a particular subject area. Do not use mass market email methods – it will backfire against your company and site. Instead, look at Chapter 7 for coverage of this exciting method of marketing, but one that needs careful consideration.

Conclusions

After the effort of planning and creating your web site, make sure that you promote it effectively to provide the greatest flow of visitors. This chapter has outlined the main techniques that you should use when actually creating your site – such as including correct index keywords – and once your site is live.

When re-launching a site, you can follow almost all of these steps. The index keywords and submissions to the main search engines will need to be adjusted, and you will need to concentrate on the benefits of your new site rather than the mere fact that it is new.

By following these steps, you will give your site the initial profile that it needs to succeed in attracting visitors in the face of competition from millions of other sites.

CHAPTER 5
Measuring response

THE key to effective marketing on the Internet, as in any other field, is the ability to measure responses to a particular campaign. Unless you are selling a product via the Internet, the only way you can measure the success of your online efforts is in increased numbers of visitors entering your web site.

In traditional fields of marketing, the only way to judge the response of a campaign is to ask the reader or viewer to respond to an advertisement. It would be wonderful if you could know the basic profile of each person who looks at your advert in a magazine – with the Internet, you can do this automatically! The access log for your web site records the source of each visitor (normally their company name and their country of origin) together with a record of the products that they viewed on your site.

By analyzing access logs and using sophisticated geotargeting tools, you can build up a picture of your online customer base and work out marketing and advertising campaigns that take this into account. If you promote a particular product with a campaign, it's easy to see the response by checking the access logs for this product's web page. This chapter covers the way in which access logs work and how best to use and analyze the records. These tools are an essential part of your marketing kit, so make sure that you are making the most of them.

Counting visitors
One of the first types of feedback devices developed for the web was the web counter. You've probably seen dozens of sites that use this feature - it's a tachometer-style counter at the bottom of the page that displays a message 'you are visitor number 1133'. Although this can be useful for a quick way of checking the popularity of your web site, it's primitive. See an example overleaf.

A web counter is a tiny little program that runs on the web server. The program is normally written in the Perl programming language that is the most popular method of writing applications running on web servers. A web counter is a very basic utility: it creates a file, then stores the number one in the file. Each time a visitor accesses the web page, the tiny program runs, reads the current number in the file and increments this. You can then display the number stored in the file to see how many people have visited your page. Or, more accurately, how many times your web page has been viewed.

You can add a counter to any page on your site. The usual place is to attach it to the main introductory page of your web site – usually called index.html – however, you can add a counter to any other page. For example, if you are launching a new product or have a special offer, you can check to see how many people visit this special offer page. (Note, it's far better to use log analysis tools, described in the next section, for this purpose.)

Let's start with one major problem of counters. If you have just launched your web site, do you really want to announce that your visitor is only the fourth person to stop by your site? Second, it shouts amateur to any visitor. Web counters are very easy to implement and offered by just about every internet provider as a free feature with every account. Lastly, they can easily give the wrong feedback to you – for example, if one person hits the Refresh button on their web browser five times, the web counter will increment five times; it doesn't know any better. Many web sites start off their web counter at, say, 5000. This gives the web site a certain air of authority and popularity, but these webmasters are doing themselves a disservice.

An alternative trick is to put a command into one page of your web site, but view the number of counts in another web page that is not linked. Since only you know the name of this 'secret' feedback page, only you can view the number in the counter. For example, if you want to monitor the general number of visitors to your site, you would put a counter command in your index.html page (the main introductory page in your web site) that would increment the counter each time a visitor looks at your web site. You would create another page called, for example, 'numbers.html' that actually displayed the results of the counter.

If you want to use a web counter in your page, you will normally need to add a line of special code to your HTML file. For example, if you want to use the free web counter script provided by the Demon Internet Service in the UK, you would add the following line in your web page:

<IMG SRC="http://www.demon.co.uk/cgi-bin/Counter.cgi?www.pcp.co.uk.index.html">

Some internet providers do not offer a web counter (all business providers should give you a web counter and an access log of visitors to your site). If you are stuck with this type of provider, but still want to count how many visitors you are attracting to your site, you can use one of the free counter services. These operate a long-distance service: you add a line of code to your web page that references the remote web counter service. This increments a counter on their computer that you can then check to see how many visitors have stopped by your site. Although the basic service is free, it often slows down your web site ~ your web page has to wait for the remote computer to respond. A well-known free service is at *www.web-counter.com.*

A better service for small companies is the free web statistics package provided by *www.showstat.com.* This also runs on a remote computer but provides much more detailed feedback about the visitors to your site. Unfortunately, part of the free deal is that all this information is available to any visitor (including your competition).

The best solution is to ignore web counters altogether and stick to a good web traffic analyzer. This will tell you exactly how many different people have visited your web site and give you a full break-down of their countries of origin, the pages on your site that they visited and much more.

Access Logs

Would you like to know in which country your customers live? Which products most interest them and what they look at when they visit your web site? You can ask all this information without ever having to trouble the customer with a clipboard or questionnaire. Every time a user visits your web site, his every action is recorded automatically in an access log. This service is provided by your internet provider (if you provider doesn't offer this basic business service, switch provider) and gives you a wealth of information

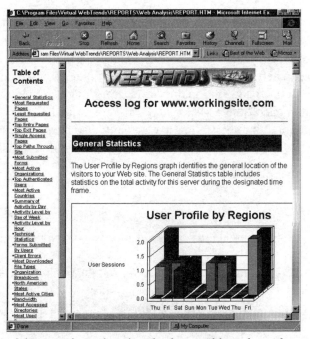

about the people that visit your site, what they look at and how long they stay; the access log is one of you best sources of information to analyse trends and response in your web

Access logs are created by special software that runs on the web server computer – normally hosted by your internet provider. This software records details of everything that the web server has to do in response to visitors accessing your web site. The log software runs automatically and stores its results in a (often very large) access log file. You can then use specialist software to analyse the information stored in these log files to find out more about the visitors to your site.

The access log really does record every single action carried out by the web server software. For example, if a user visits your web site, they will view your introductory web page that is usually called index.html. The user's web browser sends a GET request to the web server to ask for this page. The web server sends the HTML file back to the browser and waits for the next request. If your index.html page has any images, these need to be requested separately, again using GET commands. This means that one user's visit to your site can result in a dozen lines in the access log.

Each line in the access log has the time, command and file name that was requested by the user. The log also records information garnered by asking the user's web browser questions. For example, most access logs will record the type of browser that the user is running, the domain name that the user is working from and, in some cases, can also record the name of the last web site that the user visited! All this information is stored by the user's browser and, depending on the way the browser works, can be automatically reported if the access log software asks the right questions.

Reading the server access logs

The type of information recorded in an access log and the way in which this information is stored depend entirely on the access log software running on the server. In most cases, this choice is down to your internet provider, so unless you have your own in-house web server you have no say in the matter. Luckily, there are really only three main formats used to store this log information.

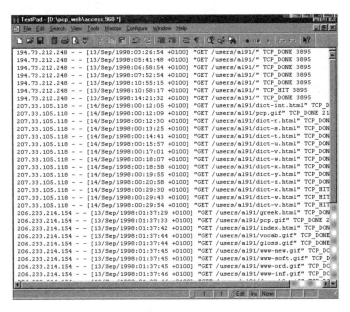

The most common access log file format follows the standard used by the NCSA web server software – normally called NCSA httpd 1.4 (the similar, and hugely-popular Apache web server software normally also uses this file format). The second file format is used by Microsoft's IIS web server software. The third type of file format encompasses the range of proprietary file formats used by less popular web server software. Try and find out the name and version of web server software that your internet provider is using – it will help you choose the correct and compatible analysis software that you'll need to analyze the results later on.

The NCSA and Apache web servers (together this accounts for around 70% of all web servers, and the majority of all ISP servers) generate an access log stored in the Common Log Format. This provides ten separate fields for each record entry and gives plenty of detailed information. To help you sort out what it all means, there are many freeware and shareware utilities that will analyze an access log, sort out its contents and provide graphs of number of visitors or hits per page.

The access log is usually stored as a plain text file and can be viewed or edited with any text editor. The ten fields within each line (or record) in a Common Log Format file are:

IP Address/Name
The full IP address of the visitor's remote host or, if it can resolved by the local DNS server, the full name of the remote host.

remote logname
Account name of the user accessing your server – if it can be retrieved from the remote host.

user
Full user name of the user accessing your server – if it can be retrieved from the remote host.

data and time
Date followed by time of the access, written as 22/May/1997 and the time in 24-hour format.

GMT adjustment
The offset from the GMT time standard according to the local server.

operation
The command that was requested by the remote user; for a web page this is always a 'Get' statement.

file
The path and name of the HTML file that contains the web page being accessed.

server protocol
TCP/IP protocol used to carry out the command – normally HTTP to access a web page.

status
Any error or status codes generated by the HTTP server; a code of 200 indicates a successful completion.

file size
Size of the file that was retrieved.

Analyzing access logs
Once your web site is active and you have asked your ISP to start recording an access log (although this normally starts automatically with business-oriented accounts), you can begin to analyze the findings. It's no exaggeration to state that good and regular analysis of web site access logs is essential to any web marketing professional.

Analysis software will help you identify key indicators that you can use to tailor your marketing strategy. For example, you can view:

- the country of origin of your visitors
- the products (or web pages) that interest particular visitors
- the success of a special offer or new product
- the source of your visitors – whether from a search engine reference or linked site
- the success of a banner ad
- response to print or email campaigns that specify a particular web page.

To help provide all these answers, you will need to use special analysis software. This works in two ways. First, you can run software on the web server to produce a report or you can run a program on your computer to produce a report. The most common solution is the first, but this means that you have to get your hands dirty running a Perl application on your internet provider's web server. It's not difficult, but if you are not comfortable typing in commands, you might prefer the second approach.

Perl-based log analysis

Perl is a programming language which is a very popular method of writing web-based applications. There is a wide range of log analysis tools available as freeware or shareware that have been written in Perl. To use this type of software, you really need a Perl interpreter which can understand the Perl program. You web server (or your ISP's web server) should provide this feature as standard, or you can download a product that will run under Microsoft Windows or DOS.

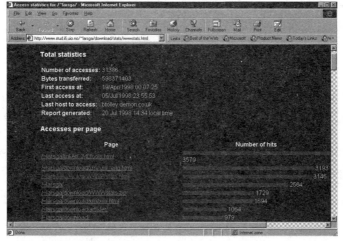

Once you have a Perl interpreter, run the Perl log analysis tool and enter the name of the file that contains the log. The analysis tool will usually produce a long report stored in HTML format which includes a break-down of different patterns and statistics relating to your visitors. You can then view this HTML report file using a web browser.

For example, here is the way that I check the access log statistics using a Perl analysis tool.

1. Telnet to my web site on my ISP's computer using a Telnet program (under Windows 95: Start/Run then enter 'Telnet' or download a shareware Telnet program from *www.shareware.com*)
2. Log into the web server.
3. Move to the directory that contains the access log – managed automatically by the ISP.
4. Type in the command to start the log analysis tool 'analog' (if your ISP does not provide this software for you, then you will need to download the analysis software from its source site then upload the software to your web site using an FTP program).
5. Start my web browser.
6. Enter the URL for the HTML file that has been produced by the log analysis tool.

You can see a whole range of access log tools by searching your favourite search engine for 'access log'. Two popular shareware software products are Analog *(www.stabslab.cam.ac.uk/~sret1/analog)* and Mktats (available from many sources, search *www.yahoo.com.* for your nearest site.)

Java-based analysis tools

As you can see, running Perl-based log analysis takes several steps. In fairness, it probably looks more complex than it really is – if you have uploaded your own web site, then a Perl analysis tool should pose no problems for you. However, there is an easier method!

The second type of analysis software is normally written as a Java program that runs within your web browser on your computer. To analyze your access log, you need to download the access log file from your web site then open your web browser and open the analyser web page stored on your local hard disk. This action will automatically start the Java software that will then display a breakdown of your access log.

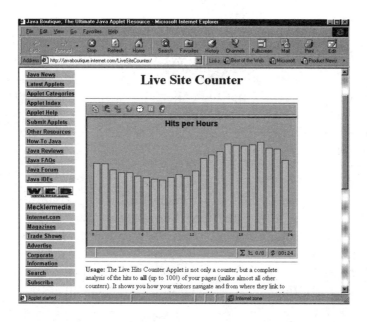

Java-based tools are easy to use, will work within any Java-capable browser and, best of all, you do not need to run Telnet or enter any commands on your web server. Their downside is that you normally have to pay for a Java tool, wheras Perl scripts are often freeware or shareware.

Most of the Java-based analysis tools produce nice three-dimensional graphs of visitor rates and can break down the log information into a wide range of categories. For example, here is the way that I check my site's log file using the Java-analysis tool:

1. Connect to the Internet, start my web browser.
2. Type in the name of the setup web file stored on my local hard disk ('c:\web\log\setup.html').
3. The Java application starts automatically, links to the my web site and analyses the log file, displaying an initial visitor graph.

There is a wide range of Java-based analysis software available, most of it very sophisticated. This software tends to be sold as commercial products and can be expensive. However, almost all suppliers provide a demonstration product that can be tried out with your data before you have to pay for the product.

Using Analysis Tools

The reports produced by access log analysis tools help you look at the raw data in different, manageable sections. The reports produced by the different tools will vary in design and presentation – some will use tables of numbers, others will create three-dimensional graphs – but the underlying data is the same.

Look at each of the separate reports – they all provide useful information that you can use to either improve the features you offer or can help you target your material more accurately to your visitors.

Geographic Location

One of the most interesting – and most misleading – reports provides you with a breakdown of users according to their geographic location. These results are derived from the two characters at the right-hand end of a domain name. For example, 'microsoft.co.uk' is based in the UK wheras 'microsoft.co.au' is based in Australia. US-based and international companies tend to prefer the '.com' suffix but this is difficult for analysis tools to assign to one specific country.

Domain name

This second report uses the same parts of the raw access log as the Geographic location report. However, this time the analysis tool totals the number of hits from each domain or host name. This gives a good idea of your customer-base. For example, if you find that the majority of your visitors are from CompuServe.com then you could consider providing local links within the CompuServe forum or finding out if there has been a good write-up or discussion about your site on a CompuServe discussion forum (similar to, but separate from internet newsgroups).

Other uses of this report are to check if your competitors have been looking at your web site – and for how long – and if there are any companies or educational institutions (both types of organization normally have their own unique domain names) that have made considerable use of your site. Again, if it is an educational domain name (with .edu in the name), then perhaps your site appears as a reference in a course or a librarian is interested in your product or someone is interested in evaluating your products.

Page requests

The most useful report that you will want to generate is one detailing the popularity of different web pages on your web site. This can give you a clear impression of how to allocate your marketing budget or how to develop new product ranges. Use this report regularly as a method of checking how promotions on less-popular products are improving visitor rates.

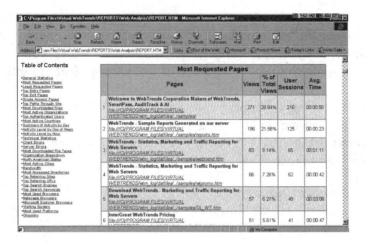

Once you have noted the most popular web pages on your site, consider adding links to these as quick short cuts from your main index page. You should always try and allow a user to reach their final destination in just three clicks, and this will speed users to their destination.

Browser type

Almost all access logs will record the type of web browser that a user is running. This might seem an odd request, but it will help you design a web site that best fits your user's requirements. For example, you can easily tell if the majority of users are running a Microsoft or Netscape web browser. Use this to make sure that you test your web pages with this brand of browser and do not use any features specific to the other brand of browser. You might find that most of your users are running older browsers (particularly if they are connecting from schools or small businesses that do not need to update software so regularly). In this case, there's no point spending money and time producing complex Java applets since these users cannot run Java.

Referring domains

An interesting report will provide a list of the web sites that were visited prior to entering your web site. For example, if you discover that the majority of your visitors were at the search engine Yahoo.com, wheras only a few percent arrived from the Excite.com search engine you will know that you should concentrate on improving your index entry at Excite and perhaps advertising at Yahoo!

This is also a good way of spotting potential partners and competitors. For example, if you see that a number of visitors come from a competitor's site, you should try and see why they entered your competitor before you – this could be down to better site marketing or good use of META tags (see Chapter 4) or a promotional offer.

Use the referring domains report to check if your site could work more closely with another company. If you discover that visitors looking for your range of language books are actually looking for a translation agency – you could suggest a link with language agencies.

Working with domain names

When a user connects to the Internet, whether through an OSP like AOL or CompuServe, or through from their home via a local Internet provider or over an office network, they will be assigned a domain name. Unless the user registers his own domain name (this covered in Chapter 1 and 8), then he will 'adopt' the Internet provider's domain name. (Note: sometimes, the domain name will be called the host name or IP dotted name or server name – they all refer to the unique name that identifies your home web site or server.)

When you connect to the Internet, you actually dial a telephone access number managed by your internet provider and then log into their gateway computer that checks that you are a registered user. From this stepping-stone, you can move on to and visit other web sites on the Internet. Your domain name will be the name given to this gateway computer.

Each server computer (not your desktop PC) that forms part of the Internet supports a set of variables that contain information about the way the server has been configured. These variables are called the server environment variables and are public and so can be read by any other computer on the Internet. In addition to these server variables, there are also a set of user environment variables that are stored by each user's web browser.

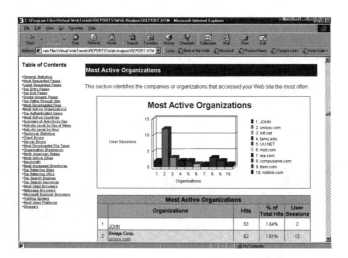

These two types of environment variables contain a range of technical information about you, your server and your software. For example, the variables can include information about the type of webserver software that is running, the type of web browser you are using, the domain name of the server, your email address, your authenticated user name and so on. Some of these variables are never set – for example, the email address is never set, otherwise anyone could find your email address. However, other variables are always set: the type of browser software you are using and the server software that is running.

For marketing purposes, we are only really interested in a few of these variables – if their content has been set. Typically, it is useful to know the type of web browser your visitor is using, their domain name and the previous site the user visited. To retrieve these variables, you would use a small Perl script that runs on your web server and interrogates (invisibly) the user's web browser when they enter your site.

You could set up a simple Perl script that checks the type of web browser a visitor is using and, if it's an older version, automatically switch to a simple text-only version of your web site. This means users connecting with an old web browser will not be troubled by your latest Javascript enhancements to your site.

For example, if you want to find out the previous web site visited by a user entering your site, you could use the Perl script (see Chapter 3 for details about how to enter and run Perl scripts):

```
#!/usr/local/bin/perl
$prev_site =$ENV('HTTP_REFERER');
print "You visited $prev_site before turning to us!", "\n");
exit (0);
```

A similarly simple script will find and print the domain name of the user:

```
#!/usr/local/bin/perl
$home_domain =$ENV('REMOTE_ADDR');
print "You are visiting from $home_domain - welcome!", "\n");
exit (0);
```

Lastly, we can create a simple Perl script that checks the type of browser that the user is running. This is a good way of ensuring that the visitor does not run into problems when trying to access new plug-ins or features on your site:

```
#!/usr/local/bin/perl
$browser_model =$ENV('HTTP_USER_AGENT');
print "You are using the $browser_model web browser.", "\n");
exit (0);
```

Many web sites now use exactly the opposite approach to this mini Perl script. They include a set of Javascript commands which direct a compatible browser to the enhanced version of the web site, leaving older web browsers that cannot run Javascript to load the plain vanilla site.

The next generation of visitor analysis

So far, I have described two types of customer analysis methods: a simple counter and more detailed log analysis. However, although the latter option, access log analysis, is used by the majority of small and medium-sized web sites, it is limited. You cannot see exactly when or how a user clicked from one page to another; it's difficult to use this mass of raw information to check different routes taken through the links on your web site.

The next generation of visitor analysis products are already available and provide far more detailed marketing information. They have been developed with similar technology that used to analyse spending patterns on store-cards and reward-cards; how special offers change spending habits in supermarkets and so on.

This new range of software really tries to show you patterns in customer behaviour rather than raw web requests. For example, if you have a web page that's heavy on graphics, some users might find it takes too long to receive and so will click the Stop button half-way through. The access log still records the original request, but you don't know that the user got fed up. You'll never know why this potential customer left your web site.

Some analysis tools are actually customer-driven and used for the benefit of the customer (although they also provide great marketing information). For example, Amazon.com – the huge online bookstore – can link different books bought by the same person. If you search for a Business Dictionary, Amazon's software provides the basic information but also tells you that previous customers also bought a Dictionary of Banking and a Dictionary of Accounting.

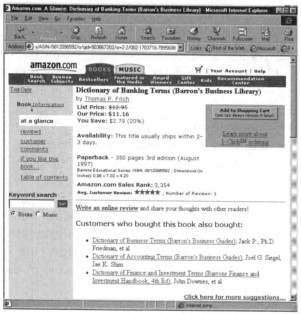

Other complex web sites allow the user to customize the content – for example, to view a particular stock porfolio or local weather and news. This information can then be used to add extra value by including advertisements or further information based on this geographic or interest-driven data. Sites such as Excite (*www.excite.com*) and MSN (*www.msn.com*) allow you to create your own custom look to get just the information that you want.

Taking this type of custom information delivery to the extreme are push channels such as Pointcast (*www.pointcast.com*). Push channels deliver news, features, weather and other information to the viewer which is then displayed either on a screen-saver or on a web browser (the PointCast system automatically downloads the latest news every hour and displays the headlines on the user's screen-saver).

The beauty of this type of system is that the user can tailor the sources and types of news and feature that he receives. For example, if you work in marketing, live in London and love wine, fashion and skiing, then you can select industry-specific news for marketing, UK news and London weather, features on wine, fashion and sports updates for skiiing. The perfect tailored-fit. The PointCast company gets an exact match for its customers and so can sell advertising that is downloaded at the same time. In this case, there could be adverts for a wine web site, cheap skiing holidays and so on. This custom information delivery provides the ultimate acceptable face of user analysis. The problem is that the programming and setup costs are very high.

Geotargetting

By using visitor analysis tools (mentioned above) to look through the raw data in your web site's access logs you can get a good idea of which pages each person visits. The ultimate is to try and find out where this person lives or is calling from. This information could give you a whole new range of marketing possibilities and provide important sales information that you can use to improve traditional marketing and advertising in a particular area or country.

Geotargetting aims to provide these answers. The simplest method is to look in the access log at the visitor's domain name. This gives you the user's company domain name or the domain name of their ISP or OSP. Unfortunately, it is hardly an exact science.

For example, if I visit a web site, the access log would record my domain name as 'pcp.co.uk'. This is perfect; I can be easily identified as being based in the UK – from the last two letters of the domain name. Unfortunately, if I am using my CompuServe account to browse the web, the access log would read 'compuserve.com' – I could be calling from the US, UK or any of the hundreds of other countries covered by CompuServe.

It gets worse. If the visitor works for a large company, such as IBM, then the company would have a firewall installed to protect its internal network from hackers. Any visitor to my web site would record the domain name of the firewall – perhaps 'firewall.ibm.com'. All these employees visiting my site, regardless of the country in which they work, would record this 'dummy' domain name.

When you start to look at your access logs, you will find that at least one quarter of all your visitors will have the domain names of the two main OSPs: AOL and CompuServe (aol.com and compuserve.com). This provides absolutely no useful geographic information. You will also find that perhaps another quarter of the visitors will have manually switched off the domain reporting function (it is voluntary), so you will have no idea of their domain name and so will have no idea of their location.

Of the remaining visitors, some will be from company or educational domains that are easy to place on a map and provide the first real geographic information. The rest will be personal or home users that do not have their own domain and instead use their ISP's domain name. For example, if you are using the NetCom ISP, your domain would be recorded as 'netcom.com'.

Clever analysis software ignores the text version of the domain name (such as 'netcom.com') and instead uses the original numerical form of the domain name. It then uses a reverse-DNS method to come up with the country in which this domain has been registered (although it ends in .com, this domain could be registered in the UK, US or any other country).

The initial ideal has quickly been whittled away to provide just a small tranche of visitors who can usefully supply geographic data based on their domain name. The goal is to try and use other analysis methods to find out the geographic location of your visitor. Some larger sites have several versions of the same web site with different localized content – the user is asked to select their home country's web site. Each country-specific site has local contact details, local pricing, special offers and so on and so makes it worth the user making this extra effort.

Another method is to try and offer features that need a geographic answer. For example, many web sites (*such as www.excite.com* and *www.msn.com*) allow users to tailor their site with the user's local weather – the user enters their zip code or city name. Now, suddenly, you have the exact location of this user. Well, maybe; if the user lives in New York but wants to visit Seattle, he will check the weather in Seattle.

Sources of information on this type of advanced customer analysis are available from vendors which include:

Accrue Software - *www.accrue.com*
DoubleClick - *www.doubleclick.com*
Intersé - *www.interse.com*
Aptex - *www.aptex.com*

Conclusions

As you can see, there are a wide range of methods that can provide customer analysis. Most web sites use the access log method to find out which web pages are most viewed. You can also sometimes find out the country of origin of the customer and the web site that they visited previously. However, if you try and read too deeply into this information, you can get the wrong answer – geotargetting shows how easy it is to get the wrong impression about the true location of your customers.

You should analyse your web access logs as a first step then provide techniques to try and find out any extra information you require. For example, adding a feedback box or allowing the user to request a printed catalogue means that they have to enter their address. If you offer a free download, ask the user to enter some of their details first (but keep it simple, such as name, country, and email address – see Chapters 3 and 6 for more details on forms and involving users).

By using all of these techniques in combination, you will soon get a much clearer picture of your customers – and see which customers log off your site. This feedback can now be used to improve marketing or products for specific customers.

CHAPTER 6
Involving the Visitor

YOUR web site should be interesting, encourage repeat visits and involve the user. If a visitor knows that your site has a lively discussion group, they will probably drop in and read the latest comments. Similarly, up-to-date news pages (trade or product news rather than world news) make it worth a repeat visit. If you can convince the visitor that your site is packed with useful information, in addition to your own product or company details, then they will be regular visitors.

To encourage visitors to come back to your site, you need to involve them in as many ways as possible. Create an environment that is dynamic and relevant – it takes some effort to set up and manage, but it will be well worth while when your access log starts to reflect the increased number of visitors. Better still, these are not just passing surfers, but regular users that have built up a trust in your company and the service you offer.

In this chapter, I will cover the different ways in which you can add interest to your web site and involve the visitors. Once you have got someone to look at your site, you want them to stay there as long as possible – look at the features, get into a discussion, find out the latest news and then use your site as a springboard to visit other related sites.

Keeping a visitor on your site
Your aim when creating a user-friendly web site is not just to create an online version of your catalogue. That's too easy and too dull. Visitors will drop by the site, have a quick look at your products and move on. The real trick is to create an 'experience' that encourages the visitor to drop in and stay a while.

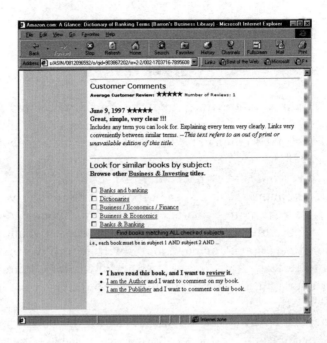

Some of the most interesting sites provide more extra related information than actual core-product details. For example, the Amazon.com (*www.amazon.com*) site has millions of books listed, but also provides author news, the chance to contribute your own review of a book and lists of the top titles. You can easily visit there looking for a book and end up spending an hour browsing book-related information. Have another look at your site's structure: are you providing a catalogue or a welcoming information source?

Discussion groups

Discussion groups provide a neat way of adding activity to your web site – with little extra effort on your part. Any visitor can contribute to the discussion group and can ask a question or reply to another user's query. Once they become popular (see Chapter 4 for ways to promote your site) the discussion group can soon generate hundreds or thousands of messages per day. Your job is to set up the infrastructure (the software) and monitor the messages. There are several ways of adding an online discussion group.

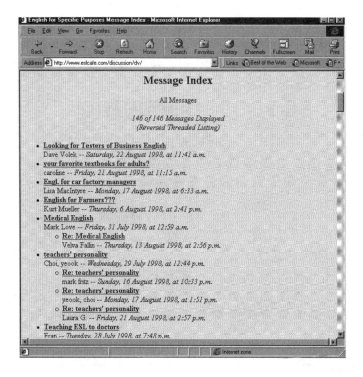

Mailing List

You can add a mailing list (often called a listserver) that distributes postings from each group member to everyone else on the list. Mailing lists are best as a means of distributing information around a large number of users and are often used for popular newsletters (see Chapter 7) and for company information.

Adding a mailing list server to your site is an excellent way of providing information to subscribers who are interested in keeping up to date with your company, products or market. Unlike a newsletter (see Chapter 7) you can provide the basic infrastructure for the mailing list and leave it to the subscribers to contribute information. Any messages posted to the mailing list by a subscriber will be circulated to all other subscribers. Plenty of educational and trade discussion groups use a mailing list.

The way a mailing list server works is simple: an application on the server holds a list of the email addresses of subscribers, when a user submits a new article it is distributed by the mail list server to all the other subscribers in the list. There are plenty of extra features that allow articles to be checked by a moderator before they are mailed out, but this is the basic function. There are tens of thousands of mailing lists already running on the internet – look at *www.liszt.com* for a detailed index of all the lists.

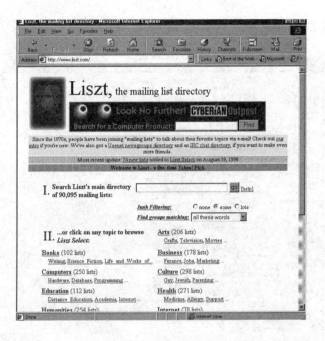

One of the most popular applications that will support a mailing list is called LISTSERV from Lsoft (*www.lsoft.com*). This server software will run on most web server platforms but it is far easier to ask your internet service provider to include this feature in your hosting package. If you have your own web server in-house, the server software should be able to support mailing list features.

The disadvantage of a mailing list is that it sends everything by email, so users do not have to visit your web site (where they would see your other products and any other advertising you have displayed).

Bulletin board

The original bulletin board started life in the company canteen – anyone could pin up a notice to arrange a meeting, organize a team or sell something. The Internet equivalent adds the same sort of functions to your web site and provides a great way of allowing visitor discussion, but keeping them on your web site (a mailing list uses email for distribution, so the subscribers don't have to visit your site again).

With a bulletin board system, any visitor can submit a message; this is stored on your web server with a title. For example, if a user wants to find a good print-shop in his district, he would type in 'Print shops in London' for the title, the main message and click submit. The new message will be stored and listed in the main group of messages. If another user reads this and wants to reply to the message, they highlight the message from the list and click Reply. Their new message now appears as an adjunct to the original. After some activity on your board, the message structure will look like a tree with original messages and branches off these for replies.

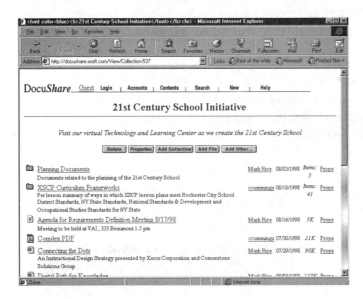

A bulletin board works using special software that runs on the web server. For most companies, this will be on their internet service provider's computer that hosts their web site. Some internet providers include a library of add-on features and you might find that you can set up a pre-configured bulletin board with no effort. However, most users will need to install their own software.

The good news is that bulletin board management software is normally written in the Perl programming language (so can run on almost every web server) and is generally offered on freeware or shareware basis. A great source for a whole range of different bulletin board software is *www.freecode.com* (it includes more than 500 freeware and shareware programs that you can use to enhance your web site).

Once you have downloaded the bulletin board management software, you will need to install it on to your web server. Read the instructions carefully – installing a Perl script differs from one internet provider to the next. You will need to use the same FTP program to upload the scripts on to your web server and then add new control tags to web pages that allow users to submit and read messages. The best solution is to ask your ISP to install the script for you. However, if you have time you can follow through the steps that are included with the software and install the product yourself.

Once the main bulletin board program is installed, you will need to create a set of web pages that work with the program. One web page will display current messages to the bulletin board and another is used to submit a message or reply to a message. Again, templates for these pages should be included with the main scripts you download.

Feedback forms

All the features that we have covered so far are directed at company to user or user to user communications. By adding a feedback form to your web site you will ensure that your visitors have the opportunity to send you comments, orders and other requests.

You should ensure that your site has at least one form allowing visitors to send comments back to you. Typically, your site might have a form to request further information, a comments form, a form in your press-room page that lets reporters request interviews or review products and, finally, an order form.

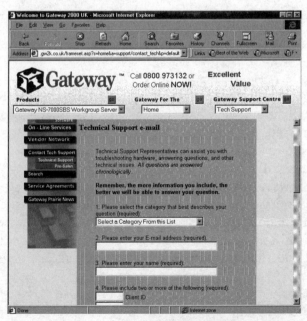

Creating a form is easy if you are using one of the newer graphical web page design programs, such as Microsoft FrontPage or Adobe PageMill. You can draw in the fields, define radio buttons or checkboxes and create a button to submit this information. Once you have the web page designed, you will need a special Perl script that runs on your web server to manage the distribution of the contents of the form – normally, this is by email. Your ISP should have a pre-written script it can send you to automate this process.

Many sites use forms to ask for registration before allowing access to a free product download or database. Try not to ask for too much information, however tempting, since this will put off many visitors. The ultimate minimalist form is often displayed on sites with a newsletter - just a single line for the user to enter their email address to request a subscription.

Guest books

A simple way to encourage users to write comments about your site is to provide a guest book. This lets your visitors tell you, and other visitors, about themselves and their thoughts on the site. This might sound like a rather flawed PR exercise, but it works successfully on some types of web site – typically those with a small, close-knit but widely-spread customer base.

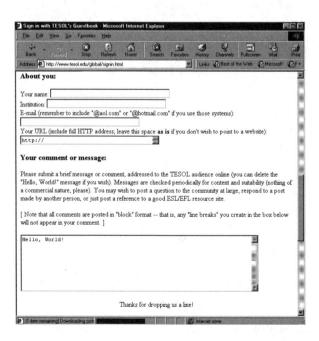

A good example are specialist teachers; they can write in a guest book where they are currently teaching, their areas of expertise and requests. A guest book feature is a nice addition – if the visitor's don't abuse it – and provides a similar forum to the bulletin board system (above) but is easier to install and operate for the web site managers. The usual way of providing a guest book function is by using Perl scripts – visit the *www.freecode.com* site for a range of free packages that you can install onto your web server.

Add-a-link

Since the internet makes it easy to skip from one site to another, it might seem odd to provide links to other sites within your site. Although this sounds like an invitation to leave your site as soon as possible, in fact users welcome a resource page that includes links to related sites. It saves them having to search for another site and provides an indication to the user that you are confident in your products and site. In general, adding a resource page will help repeat visits – you are now a resource centre – rather than encouraging visitors to leave.

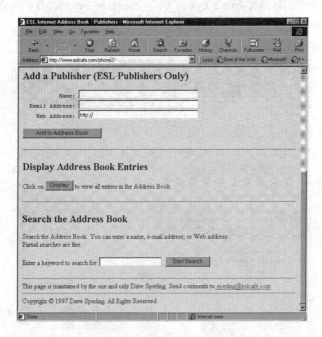

You can create your own resource page and include links to related useful sites and pages – to your distributor, trade organizations, software and book pages. However, it can soon take up all your time trying to add to this list of online resources. The simple solution is to let your users do the work!

Web sites featuring a strong sense of community spirit provide comprehensive resource pages and normally allow a visitor to add a new entry to the resource page. This feature, normally called add-a-link, works using a Perl script (again, visit the *www.freecode.com* site for free examples) that runs on your web site and manages a file of links with their description.

Entries in the resource file can then be displayed on a separate web page in categories and, if the script allows, provides a search function that helps a visitor find a particular site.

Database
Linking a database to the web site helps provide an interactive element to the site. Users can search for information using a customised search form and a special search program (running on your web server) searches through the database and formats the results for display on a results web page.

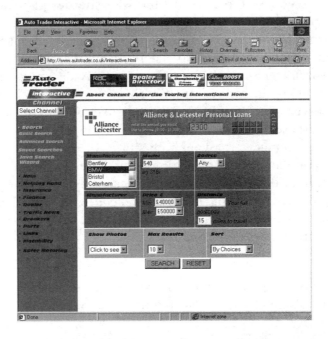

Almost every major web site has some form of database. Some are complex systems, such as the complete Yellow Pages telephone directory (at *www.yell.co.uk* in the UK and *www.bigyellow.com* in the US). Other custom sites include the AutoTrader classified car magazine (*www.autotrader.co.uk*) that lets you search for a car by make, model and price. Larger sites organize their product support databases to let visitors search for tips or answers based on a product or problem.

You can link your existing company database directly to your web site with minimal effort if you have your own web server in-house. For example, if you use the Lotus Notes information management system, you can add the Lotus Domino database publisher software and you have created a web site with full, interactive access to your company's database. Some companies, including advertising agencies, provide this as a password-protected feature for their clients, giving the client full access to the work-in-progress of any campaign.

However, adding a database to a web site needs to be planned carefully. If you have your own in-house web server, you will need to ensure that your security is up to scratch to prevent any access to your company's data, but still provide easy access from a visitor on the web site. If you are using an internet service provider to host your web site, you have several options. Many business-oriented ISPs will provide links to a database and manage the programming required – for a fee. Some web site management tools, notably Microsoft Frontpage and ColdFusion, allow you to integrate a database directly into the web site design – however, the ISP needs to install special control software to support these features.

Many business-oriented ISPs provide pre-configured search engines that you can use within your web site. Many use the same search engine that is used on the vast Excite search engine (*www.excite.com*) to provide a personal search engine for your site. ISPs using the Microsoft IIS web server to run their systems can provide its index server – a search engine provided by Micorosoft. If your ISP provides either of these solutions, then it is very simple to provide a full search feature over all the documents on your web site.

The most popular method of adding a database feature is to use one of the many free Perl scripts that provide database searching. There are dozens of free and shareware products listed on the *www.freecode.com* site that help database management. The database can be a simple company contact list or a more complex list of product details with images and text.

Maps

A surprising, but very popular, use of the web is to provide instant mapping of a part of a city. For example, you can search detailed maps of the UK and USA and zoom in on a city to street level. Travel sites (such as Excite travel *www.excite.com*, Yahoo travel *www.yahoo.com* and Expedia *www.expedia.com*) provide travellers with instant mapping to help them find hotels, restaurants and attractions in a city.

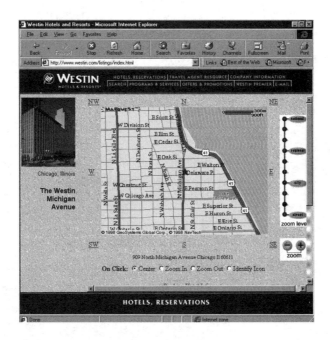

The computing power to manipulate the graphical map information is considerable – and is provided by specialist geo-mapping companies (such as *www.geosys.com*) using high-performance hardware. However, they will provide custom maps (for a modest fee) that you can add to your site – to help visitors find the office or showroom or simply as a local guide.

Conferencing and chat server

Mention chat to a savvy internet user, and they immediately think of Internet Relay Chat (IRC) that has become rather infamous as a way of arguing or even dating over the net. The problem with IRC is that the users need command-line applications that display chat text from others in a group.

The good news is that chat has been brought right up to date with new techniques and software and is now widely used for live guest appearances on web sites. Publishing companies host live chat sessions with best-selling authors and readers; it's also used by businesses instead of video conferencing to provide a forum for employees around the world to meet online without spending a fortune on air fares. New chat software works with your web browser to make interactive, real-time chat possible, friendly and fun.

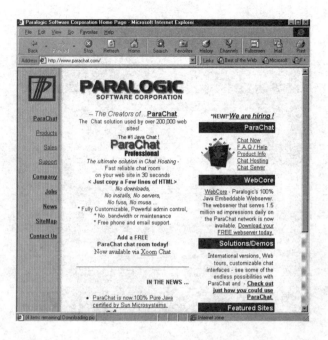

To run a chat session you can set up your system in one of two ways: one model requires the user to download a special Java applet that is run within the web browser and manages the chat sessions. The second model requires you to install special software on your web server to run the chat sessions. In both models you can set up special 'rooms' that allow users to talk about a particular subject in a room.

The two first software companies to provide chat software were Itropolis (with its iChat solution - *www.ichat.com*) and Proxicom's rival solution (*www.proxicom.com*). Not surprisingly, both Netscape and Microsoft have launched products that allow users to participate in chat or discussion forums from within their web browser.

Conferencing and chat servers

NAME	URL
ChatWare	www.eware.com
Commercial Internet System (Microsoft)	www.microsoft.com
Community System (Netscape)	home.netscape.com
ichat (Itropolis)	www.ichat.com
The Palace Commercial Server	www.thepalace.com
paraCHAT (Paralogic)	parachat.webpage.com
Proxicom Forum	www.proxicom.com

Once your chat server is running, you can create live chat or discussion sessions on your web site. These provide a great draw for visitors and give every visitor the chance to quiz the celebrity or technical guru (the two current favourite chat guests).

Broadcasting news

One of the most fashionable technologies within the internet at the moment is 'push' technology. This allows a user to ask a broadcast (or push) site to send him exactly the information he requires whenever new material is published. A good example of this sort of technology is the PointCast news system that sends you a custom newspaper: you choose the news topics you want covered, the sports events and teams to cover and the magazine features and weather area you want to hear about.

A similar system to push is the channel concept developed by Microsoft and Netscape within their web browsers. A user can 'subscribe' to a channel that is then displayed on the user's web browser in a separate window. The window is updated regularly from the main broadcast site. Sites that provide channels vary from news and magazine sites to software companies that keep you informed about software product releases.

If you want to use the same technology that drives the PointCast news delivery system, visit the BackWeb web site to find out about this broadcast system (*www.backweb.com*). Alternatives to BackWeb is Marimba's Castanet (*www.marimba.com*) software that lets you set up as a test broadcaster to see if your service works and is viable before you pay a licence fee.

Calendars and schedules

One unexpected use of the Internet is as a method of delivering a calendar and diary to a group of users. The calendar is stored on the web server and each authorised user can view the diary, add appointments and schedule meetings. This is a great way of providing a link with your key distributors or customers and, if linked in to a private area of your web site, could help closer ties with the partner and promote an open working environment.

Many commercial web sites include a calendar feature to display key dates or release schedules to any visitor. In this case, the system is a basic program (normally a Perl script) that runs on the web server and displays a standard month-to-view display. The important dates for conventions, product release and so are provided by the site managers. This feature is particularly useful for organisations that coordinate meetings around the country or have splinter groups needing a centralised diary.

There are several calendar products available – including freeware and shareware scripts – that you can use to improve scheduling on your site. Visit the *www.freescript.com* sit for the range of scripts available. If you have your own web server, your server software might already support this feature. For example, the Lotus Notes/Domino server set up makes it easy to provide web-ready calendars (*www.lotus.com*). Netscape's Calendar server runs on its web server software (*www.netscape.com*) and Microsoft's IIS web server can work with its Exchange groupware server to provide published diaries (*www.microsoft.com*) as can Novell's GroupWise product (*www.novell.com*).

Live sound, video & multimedia

The new trend in multimedia web sites is to provide synchronised multimedia delivery, including real time video, sound and animation. If you want to provide a live link to a television broadcast or a simultaneous transmission of an interview, then this type of system could be the solution. Many companies use the live sound transmission to broadcast radio over the web. Other companies have used this medium to broadcast a video and sound interview with a president or CEO – to reporters or key customers. Lastly, if you want to demonstrate a new product to key accounts or journalists, you can provide a live video link as the product is put through its paces.

Established technologies, such as RealAudio, provide excellent real time audio delivery from a web site and are often used to broadcast live radio, concerts or interviews over the net. For video, there are several standards that deliver video content to a web page.

The new goal is to provide the same sort of combination of multimedia that has made interactive CD-ROMs so popular. If these new technologies can be perfected, you could soon see the web being used to deliver interactive multimedia teaching, tours and training.

Current technologies, such as RealAudio, rely on the web server to transmit the data – however, web server is designed to send data when it is ready, rather than sending a regular stream of data that is required by multimedia. If you have ever tried to view a video clip over the Internet, you will have encountered this burst-transmission problem: when traffic or server load lightens, you get high-speed video, when the server is busy, you can watch the frames roll by each minute. To provide a good multimedia server, the data delivery must be regulated and ideally synchronised.

There are many different standards being used to deliver sound and video over the Internet and each is adapting to provide better service. For example, RealAudio is now in release 3 that can be set up to provide a single source for a group of users to reduce bandwidth requirements and improve the quality of the finished transmission. Progressive Networks (developers of RealAudio) is also working on its multimedia delivery standard, RealMedia Architecture (RMA).

There are many different standards being used to deliver sound and video over the Internet and each is adapting to provide better service. For example, RealAudio is now in release 3 that can be set up to provide a single source for a group of users to reduce bandwidth requirements and improve the quality of the finished transmission. Progressive Networks (developers of RealAudio) is also working on its multimedia delivery standard, RealMedia Architecture (RMA).

The big server developers are also working on new technologies: Microsoft includes the NetShow server (that supports both audio and video) and Netscape has its MediaServer product that does not support video, but offers more sophisticated links than the Microsoft product. Like RMA, MediaServer supports a wide range of mixed media and can synchronise these with Java applets on delivery using its new LiveAudio delivery format. Each of these technologies allow the manager to limit the delivery of data to a maximum data rate, which would eliminate the problem I mentioned earlier of a rush of video data!

Microsoft's own new multimedia delivery format, ASF (active streaming format) is supported by its own NetShow product and has support from existing products such as Macromedia, VDOnet, Vivo, and VXtreme. The latter, VXtreme format, provides a new streaming video delivery via its WebTheater product using adaptive forecasting to try and deliver the best possible quality video at a reasonable frame rate.

Multimedia servers

NAME	AUDIO	VIDEO	URL
Media Server (Netscape)	yes	no	home.netscape.com
NetShow (Microsoft)	yes	no	www.microsoft.com
RealMedia (Progressive Networks)	yes	yes	www.realaudio.com
StreamWorks (Xing)	yes	yes	www.xingtech.com
VDOLive (VDOnet)	yes	yes	www.vdo.com
WebTheater (VXtreme)	yes	yes	www.vxtreme.com

Multilingual considerations

The majority of internet users might well be based in the US, but the rest of the world is getting connected and appreciates local language considerations. One of the best ways to involve a non-English speaking visitor is to provide different language versions of your site or, ideally, localized sites for each main country in your territory.

The first consideration is to provide translations of your web text. If you have an in-house translation department, make sure that they realise the limitations within web page design (Roman characters with accents – as used in much of

Western Europe and the US can be represented very easily on the web). Different scripts, such as Cyrillic or Japanese script characters need special font files to be installed on the user's computer.

Many translation agencies have realised the potential of handling web pages and the often short texts within them. Some services offer a quick email-based turnaround (see the Yahoo.com section under languages:translation).

If you want to make your web site as local as possible, consider registering local domain names. For example, the .com suffix is normally used by US-based companies. A .co.uk suffix shows a UK site (or localised UK site), similarly with .co.jp for Japan and so on.

When localising the web page design, do not forget to check the local dominant computer system. In the US and UK the majority of users log in with a PC running Windows wheras in France, the Apple Macintosh is very strong. Other local conditions may apply, for example in some Central European countries the telephone system is erratic and there are few ISPs, so business users often turn to a global OSP such as CompuServe. Make sure that your site does not use features not yet supported by the CompuServe – bundled web browser software.

- provide own-language versions of web pages
- do not forget to translate text in images and buttons!
- use own language captions, 'Deutsch' not 'German'
- provide local country contact details, pricing and product availability
- consider registering with a local domain name

Conclusions

There is a world of difference between a static web site acting as a simple catalogue for your company's products, and an interactive, informative web site that involves the user. Visitors are far more likely to stay and browse and, importantly, return to your web site if you provide extra features that add interest and involve the visitor.

Discussion groups and bulletin boards provide a way of letting users create an online community where they can discuss a particular subject area – your products or industry. Feedback forms ensure that visitors can let you know how they feel about their products – better than venting their frustration in a public newsgroup – and for ordering products or extra information.

Create a resource page that has links to other sites of interest to your visitors – provide an add-a-link feature so that they can contribute worthwhile sites. Linking a database lets users search custom data – from classifieds to guide books, product news to support tips.

More advanced sites could use calendaring features to provide online diaries of conventions or other important dates. Some of the bigger companies might use the multimedia delivery systems to promote or demonstrate a new product via live sound and video. Lastly, a push news service or channel will ensure that subscribers are kept up to date with your supply of news.

Whichever of these features your select to enhance your site, they will all help involve the visitor and turn your site into an information resource that has its own regular visitors and community rather than a dry, static catalogue. I know which one I would prefer to visit!

CHAPTER 7
Direct Marketing

DIRECT marketing provides an excellent way of reaching a targeted audience. It works well with the traditional postal system and you can buy mailing lists of potential customers by name, profession, income or any other criteria. Almost everyone now receives a regular supply of direct mail shots through the post each morning. If you don't like the mail, throw it away.

Imagine the effect of sending out not just a few thousand, highly-targeted letters, but several million – to everyone in a city. The postal service would get clogged up, the consumers would get suspicious and it would cost you a small fortune in postal costs. In the early days of the Internet, this is exactly what happened. The theory was, if it costs just as much to send one hundred emails as to send one million, why not send as many as possible?

Unfortunately, the Internet is a very immediate, pro-active consumer-response medium. If people do not like something, then they tend to say what they think. The other drawback is that, with the exception of the US – where local calls are free – the process of logging on and downloading your email will be costing the consumer. Into this hot-tempered, loud marketplace, some direct email marketeers decided to send out blanket email messages – called spamming. The response was first outrage then revenge!

The consumers who received the unsolicited email messages replied (the sender's address was normally indicated in early spam mail) with vicious hate-mail – called flaming the sender. This sudden, huge torrent of email traffic blocked up entire sections of the Internet infrastructure and, as a result, web access and commercial traffic was held up. The company got an instant reaction to its mail messages, the product or service was known – and hated – and it had cost them nothing. Until their internet service provider disconnected their internet account.

This scenario soon became a common occurrence. In fact, everyone on the Internet probably gets several spam email messages in their postbox each morning. As a result, direct email marketing has gained an ugly reputation.

Unsolicited mass mailing

This type of blanket email message sent to hundreds of thousands or millions of randomly-picked (or generated) email addresses. The recipients have not asked for the message and will probably delete it immediately. Some will reply with a flame message; very few will take note of the contents.

There are several companies that will supply database files with millions of email addresses, and many software products can scour the web for email addresses (the software automatically checks every web page and removes any email address links it finds, storing them with a cross-reference to the site's title or subject).

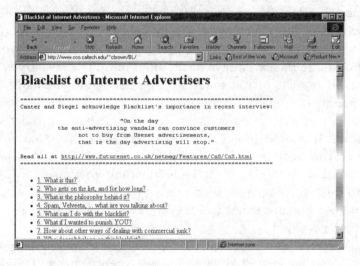

You should not, under any circumstances, resort to this type of mass mailing. At best, no one will read the message; at worst, you will damage your reputation and you could be thrown off the Internet by your provider.

Many email software products running on a user's computer can detect spam and – as a user – you can set it to reject spammed mail. Similarly, most of the main email post office sites that do the donkey work of transferring messages over the Internet are now being fitted with anti-spam features.

The trick is that most spammed mail is sent via an anonymous host. That is, there is no return or originating user named in the mail message (rather odd, if you remember that the company is trying to promote a product and its services). The reason for this is that it prevents the sender being bombarded with flame-messages. It also makes it a little more difficult to detect who is sending spam mail. However, many programmers and network managers watch out for this type of anonymous bulk mail and trace it back to a particular internet service provider, then block all mail from this provider.

Semi-researched mailing

This rather vague title refers to more targeted mail shots, but it is still unsolicited mail. You can record email addresses from newsgroup postings, mailing list postings or chat sessions. For example, if you want to mail English teachers about new classroom equipment, you could look at the newsgroup postings in the alt.education newsgroups and subscribe to the English teacher-specific mailing lists. However, the recipients will probably not appreciate having their email addresses copied in this way.

Although the mail will be unsolicited and not personalised, you can add some softer edges: for example, start the message 'dear xxx newsgroup reader' or mailing list member. At least in this way, the recipient will know how you got their address.

On a related point, the ideal would be to automatically record the email address of every visitor to your web site using access log tools. This is simply not possible (see Chapter 5 for more information). You can usually record the user's domain name (and so their general location) but you cannot get the individual's address at this domain without specifically asking for it.

Personalised mail

This is the ultimate email marketing. The recipient is willing to accept email from you about the subject in question. They have volunteered their email address and will read the messages. For example, you can ask visitors to your web site to leave their email address to be kept up to date with new product releases. You might ask that customers who buy a product from you register before they can receive support – and this involved supplying their email address.

Most web sites have general information mail addresses such as 'info@myCompany.com'. Record the addresses of visitors who send you mail. Lastly, you can buy or rent mailing lists from other web sites or agencies. These lists contain users who are happy to receive mail about a particular subject and do not mind this type of mild-spamming.

Marketing by Email

If you are using direct mail via the postal service or a telemarketing system, you should start to plan and build your direct email marketing system. Over the next year, email marketing will make serious inroads into these traditional methods of delivering messages – and you need to be ready.

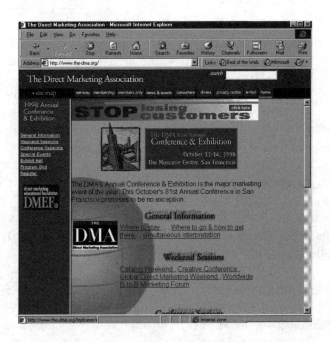

The advantages of marketing by email sound fantastic: the service is, essentially, free and the delivery is immediate. There's no chance that the mailing piece will be thrown away by a secretary and the information will be delivered right in front of the customer. Compare this with traditional direct mail or telemarketing: both take time and cost money to carry out. You can set up and send out a direct email campaign with no special equipment or software, just a standard email program, a link to the Internet and a list of email addresses.

Direct email marketing is a good way to manage on a regular basis ....
- mail press releases to your list of journalists (see Chapter 10 for more information on agencies that can do this)
- send out sales information to distributors or a sales force
- send update information to existing customers
- cold-sell a new product to a selected range of users
- create and mail out a regular newsletter or bulletin.

Best of all, an email campaign effectively puts the recipient in control. If they do not want to hear from you, they can create a rule to automatically delete any mail received from you. If they want to respond, it's as quick as clicking the Reply button. If you include hyperlinks to further details on your web site, the recipient can double-click on the hyperlink (within their email program) and move straight to your web site.

Collecting Email addresses

The first, and most important, job is to start collecting email addresses. Without a database of addresses, you will never be able to keep in touch with your customer base. There are three ways in which you can compile a list of email addresses, and you need to make sure that you are at least working on ways to use all three.

1. Recording email addresses

Do you have email at the moment? If so, have you been writing to customers, replying to questions or working with distributors? Have you added each new mail address to your email database? When someone sends you an email, you should record the address and classify it (customer, lead, etc).

Almost all the main email programs available (such as Pegasus, Outlook and Eudora) will let you build an email address book. Alternatively, make sure that your contact manager is email-aware (such as GoldMine, Act! or Organizer) and add addresses to this.

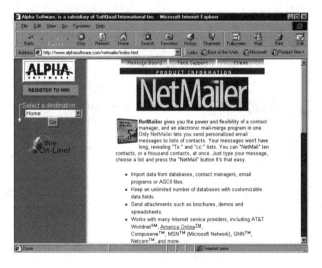

Both these solutions are good for small mailing lists, but if you have a larger list with thousands of addresses then you should consider a specialist email product such as Campaign (*www.arialsoftware.com*), NetMailer (*www.alphasoftware.com*).

2. Asking for email addresses

It sounds simple, but one of the most effective ways of getting a list of email addresses is to ask visitors to your web site to fill in a simple form. There are a few basic rules to make this system more attractive to visitors (no one likes to be told or forced to fill in a form!).

Add a one-line form on your web site main page – it could be as simple as 'Keep me posted with new product news'. No complicated questions, just a request for an email address. This approach normally works best for newsletters, but if your products are regularly updated, your customers might appreciate notification.

An alternative is to provide a more complicated form that asks the visitor to specify the information that they want to receive (newsletter, product updates, company news) and an email address.

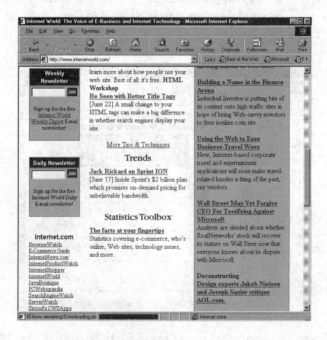

Include a feedback page on your web site – call it 'Contact Us' or similar and make sure that there are full postal, telephone and email contact details. Make it easy for the visitor – provide a simple form that asks them what information they want to know and automatically sends this as an email (the visitor doesn't even have to start his email software).

PRIVACY AND EMAIL ADDRESSES

If you plan to gather email addresses in this way and then offer them for re-sale or rent to other companies, make sure that your form includes a checkbox that allows the user to specify that he does not want to receive unsolicited mail. Respect this, or you will damage your own company's reputation.

The best advice is to print a note of what you will do with the user's contact details. If you will never sell the list, say so. If you might sell the list to advertisers, mention this. You should look at the privacy notes supplied by your Advertising Trade Standards Office or, since the majority of online users are based in the US, look at the US-based Direct Marketing Association guidelines (*www.the-dma.org*).

---

3. Hire a list of addresses

In just the same way that you can rent or buy a list of postal addresses, you can rent lists of email addresses. However, make absolutely certain that you are buying from a reputable agent and that the list is highly targeted. Do not use bulk mailing lists of random email addresses – it will backfire on you!

Look at the Yahoo Direct Marketing:Direct Email section for web-based agencies or visit the excellent *www.everythingemail.com* resource site. Agency sites such as *www.postmasterdirect.com* have lists of opt-in email addresses available. Before you use the list, ask some questions:

- how were the addresses gathered? Make sure that these are people who filled in a form at another site, not random addresses pulled by a robot from web sites
- did the addressee ask to receive information (called an 'opt-in' user)? Make sure that the people have specified that they are happy to receive more mail about a product or technology
- how old are the addresses? Mail addresses change very quickly!

Web sites such as *www.everythingemail.com* or *www.copywriter.com/lists* contains links to brokers that hold thousands of lists of 'opt-in' users. Alternatively, look at the Yahoo/marketing/direct mail/email sections – but watch out for bulk email vendors.

Mass email marketing

I have not covered mass email marketing in this book because it is not a respected, valued or productive marketing method on the internet. There are plenty of list brokers that will sell you a CD- ROM with millions of email addresses, all you need to do is include within your mail software and click send. Voila, you have successfully annoyed several hundred thousand users!

The alternative is to use address sourcing products. These will hunt through newsgroups and retrieve the email address of the poster. They will also search through online systems such as AOL or CompuServe and produce a list of users and their email addresses. Again, all these products can be found by searching for 'bulk email marketing' in your favourite search engine. Be aware, these are underhand methods of getting email addresses and, if you use them, will cause you more problems than benefit.

Lastly, there are special bulk mail products that work with a list of email addresses. These are specifically written to 'hide' the location of the sender. For example, if you send out 1m mail messages about your new ProductX, you don't want 1m angry mail messages in your mailbox. You

Sending targeted email

Now that you have your list of email addresses – a targeted list of your customers or a rented list of 'opt-in' users – you can send them your regular update or marketing item. If you have a small list, of hundreds of addresses, then your existing general email software will work fine. Use the distribution list function (for example, the free Pegasus email software includes a powerful list function that can support several different lists each with hundreds of addresses).

For larger mail-shots, of thousands of addresses, consider using a specialist mail program that can manage these larger lists. In fact, you can link your Microsoft Access database to Outlook and use this to manage mail delivery. The alternative is to use products such as NetMailer (*www.alphasoftware.com*) or Campaign (*www.arialsoftware.com*) that provide dedicated mail management software or visit the *www.everythingemail.com* resource site for further information about software applications available.

The drawback of both of these systems is that they will send their messages over your standard dial-up internet connection. This is fine if you have just a few messages to transfer, but could take hours to transfer thousands of messages. For large lists, particularly newsletters or bulletins, with tens of thousands of addresses, you should look to a server-based list server product (normally called a majordomo or listserver). These run on the computer at your internet service provider – freeing up your standard dial-up link. All you need to do is provide the data file of addresses and the text for the message, and the software does the rest.

If you have your own web server in-house, you can install your own majordomo software on the server. There are several shareware and freeware products; the most popular is probably MajorDomo (available from *www.majordomo.com* and freeware sites such as *www.freescript.com*). If you use an ISP to host your web site, you can ask them to setup a listserver program – they will probably charge a modest monthly rental fee. Lastly, if your ISP does not offer this facility, you can hire a company to manage the list for you, such as *www.sparklist.com* (search Yahoo/internet for other suppliers) or use one of the free listserver services such as *www.listbot.com* that will deliver your mail to users, but will add a line of advertising.

Newsletters
One of the best ways of establishing a relationship with your customers is to provide a newsletter. If you want to create a hit-list of potential sales prospects, use email lists and mail shots, but if you are in it for the long term then a regular newsletter or bulletin is a great technique.

An email newsletter provides a regular update to the user about a niche field – it could be topic-specific, like the excellent marketing newsletter from WilsonWeb (*www.wilsonweb.com*) or company-specific, providing information about your company and its products.

Users who want to subscribe to your newsletter enter their email address on to a form on your web site – or send a 'subscribe' email request to an automated list management program. Then, each week or month your newsletter is delivered to all the members on the mailing list.

How often should I publish?

Do not try and aim too high. Producing a regular newsletter takes a huge amount of effort; a one-off is easy, but if you promise the subscribers detailed information every week, you will need a team of writers and editors.

Perhaps the best advice is to start slow: if you are producing a company-specific bulletin, promise updates when there is news to cover or a new product launch. If you produce a more general newsletter, why not start with publication every two months. If it's a roaring success and you have plenty to write about, adjust the schedule to a monthly delivery.

Perhaps the best advice is to start slow: if you are producing a company-specific bulletin, promise updates when there is news to cover or a new product launch. If you produce a more general newsletter, why not start with publication every two months. If it's a roaring success and you have plenty to write about, adjust the schedule to a monthly delivery.

Planning a newsletter

Writing a newsletter takes just the same time and planning as any regular print bulletin – but it can be more immediate and run to tighter deadlines (since there are no production delays). Set aside a specific time a week before publication to work out the contents and structure. Research and write the feature and add news, updates and any hyperlinks.

There are two main types of newsletter that you can provide to your customers – a discussion newsletter and an announcement newsletter. A discussion newsletter is normally called a discussion group or mailing list; messages created by any subscriber are circulated around all subscribers for discussion. This type of newsletter is usually used within a discussion environment, so it is covered in Chapter 6. An announcement newsletter does what it says – it is a one-way vehicle between you and the subscribers. This type of list does not support discussion between subscribers and is more typical within marketing newsletters.

Formatting the newsletter

There is a great temptation to use the latest technology when creating email newsletters, however this can cause the majority of users (who are still happily using older technology) a lot of problems. The main temptation for an email newsletter is the arrival of HTML email. This allows email messages to contain formatting, fonts, colours and so on (often called rich-text). The newest email software, including Outlook and new versions of Eudora and Pegasus, all support formatted email messages, but older versions do not.

You have two options: if you want to appeal to all subscribers, write your newsletter as a plain text file. This will work on all email software and, although it looks rather dry, will get through. The second option is to give the user the option of subscribing to one of two mailing lists: one supplies the copy in plain format, the other supplies nicely formatted email messages (the daily email news service, *www.infobeat.com*, uses this system to good effect).

Most users are not always sure if their software supports a particular feature, such as formatted email. When a new user subscribes to your newsletter, it's a good idea to start them off on the basic text version but add a line at the bottom giving details of the formatted list. Phrase it by email software rather than by feature, for example 'If you are using Microsoft's Outlook 98, you could see this newsletter in full colour – click here to change your subscription to our formatted text edition'.

SWITCH OFF YOUR SMART FEATURES
Many wordprocessors now have smart features built in. These will automatically convert quotation marks to 'smart' curly quotes, convert fractions to symbol characters and change groups of letters (such as [c]) to a copyright symbol. All these features save time when typing, but will probably be shown as numeric codes on a user's email package. Switch off the smart features and save your newsletter or direct mail piece as a plain text file. Check that the listserver software does not interpret any special codes for internal use (many have sets of control codes that you might inadvertantly include in a document).

Send the newsletter to yourself as an exercise to check that the text looks as expected before sending it out to your thousands of subscribers.

Writing the newsletter

The Internet culture has created readers with super-short attention spans. Make your message short, punchy and – if possible – lively. A dry style is fine for the company report that is stored on your web site, but your newsletter will be read if it is interesting, informative and easy to read.

When writing, bear in mind the following guidelines – they will help you create a readable newsletter:

- start each newsletter with a short contents summary describing what is in the different parts of the newsletter
- write brief articles that are easy to digest. Include hyperlinks to more detailed information, images and so on stored on your web site
- try and include case studies, how-to or tip-and-tricks in each newsletter to help the reader work better or learn something new
- include references to historical text or articles (using hyperlinks)
- finish each issue with: a copyright notice, email contact for further information and simple instructions that explain how the subscriber can stop receiving the newsletter.

Mailing the newsletter

If you have just a few hundred subscribers to your newsletter, you can manage the entire process using standard email software (as described earlier in this chapter under direct email marketing). If a new subscriber sends in a request to join the list, you can add the users manually (or automatically, if your mail software supports automatic rules and logic) to the main distribution list. For each issue, start the email software and it will dial up your internet provider and send each user a copy of the newsletter. As you can imagine, this soon gets tedious and very time-consuming.

The ideal way to manage a newsletter is to use a special piece of software called a listserver (also known as 'listserv' or mailing list or majordomo software). This software usually runs on your internet service provider's computer or, if you have your own web server in-house, on your server.

The listserver software automatically manages the list of subscribers, accepts requests from users to join or leave this list and edits the list accordingly. All you have to do is send the newsletter original to the listserver software and it will distribute it to all users.

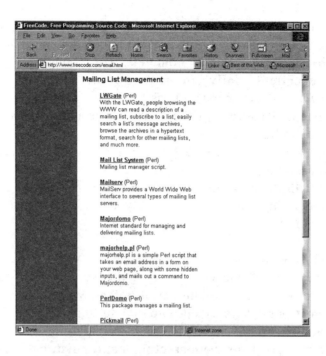

To setup a listserver, ask your ISP. They should be able to provide this function for a modest monthly fee. Alternatively, you can install the software as a Perl script in your web space (see Chapter 3 for more details), but this tends to be tricky and is best left to Perl-experts. Lastly, if your ISP does not offer this feature, you can use a commercial agency that does the work for you.

Once you have setup your listserver, all control is via email. All instructions to join or leave the list are managed by sending specially-formatted email messages to the main email address for the listserver. For example, a typical message from a user to subscribe to your list would be sent to '*listserv@listserver.myCompany.com*' and would contain the words 'subscribe myList' as the body of the message. If you have several lists (for example, one plain text, one formatted) these could be accessed by sending 'subscribe myList2' and so on. The listserver control software recognises the subscribe command and records the email address of the person sending the message.

To prevent dummy subscriptions or wrong email addresses, many list-servers now send out an acknowledge-request email that you have to reply to in order for the subscription process to complete. For example, if you want to subscribe to the excellent daily internet newsletter from Internet World (*www.internetworld.com*) the scenario is as follows:

1. type in your email address in the form on the *www.internetworld.com* web site, click the Go button,
2. the listserver sends you an email at the address you entered asking you to reply to the message,
3. if you reply with the message text 'ok' the subscription is completed and you will start receiving the newsletter. If you do not reply, the subscription request is ignored.

Managing subscribers

When running a newsletter, you want to try and ensure that anyone who wants to subscribe can do so with the least amount of bother. When newsletters started out on the internet, most publishers asked potential subscribers to fill in a long, complicated form detailing their name, address, occupation and a range of other information. This was great for the marketing mailing list, but – as I mentioned at the start of this section - newsletters are best when used for building a long-term trusted relationship rather than raw data gathering.

The current standard method is to ask a potential subscriber for the minimum information required – just their email address. Typically, you could add a small box on your main web site that suggests visitors might want to subscribe to your regular newsletter. Below this is a short field in which the visitor can enter their email address and a button to submit the application. Easy.

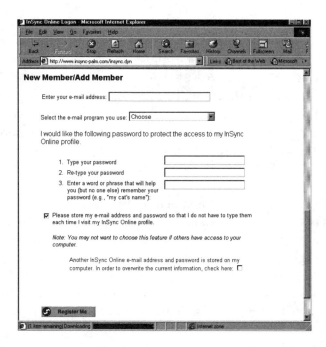

Once the user has submitted their application, it is routed to your listserver software (see above) that will add the address to the main list according to the type of list that you want to run. There are three types of subscription system that you can support: Open, closed and confirmed.

In an open system, anyone can subscribe to a list by sending an email that says 'subscribe myList'; the listserver software sends back a confirmation message and the person is subscribed. Since the person subscribed themselves, there's no chance of being accused of spamming or sending unsolicited junk mail.

In a closed subscriber system, anyone can ask to subscribe, but the listserver software will send the request on to you, the list manager, for approval before the user's name is added. This is good for paid subscription services.

In a confirmed subscriber system, any one person can subscribe any other person. For example, I can type in my colleague's email address. However, the listserver software will send this nominated person an email message to confirm that they do want to be subscribed before continuing. This is unusual, but can be useful when dealing with a trusted group of users.

Advertising in a newsletter

An announcement newsletter is normally created for marketing purposes. Discussion newsletters (or discussion groups) are created for general chat with no commercial motive (see Chapter 6). Because of this, most subscribers will realise that your announcement newsletter will have some message or purpose. For example, if you subscribe to the InfoBeat email newspaper (*www.infobeat.com*), the first few lines are taken up with a short marketing message from a sponsor. If you have created your newsletter to promote your company by providing industry or related information, you can safely add advertisement text or blatant plugs for your products.

If your newsletter is being snapped up by subscribers (that is, you get over 10,000 subscribers on a regular basis) you could consider selling ad space within each issue. The advertiser gets a highly-targeted newsletter with a known subscriber count; you get sponsorship for each issue. Unlike banner advertising on a web site, the message on a newsletter will have to be text-based and is generally low-key in tone. Most sponsors use an offer or promotion to lure readers to their web sites. See Chapter 9 for more information on how to buy and sell ad space in a newsletter.

Conclusions

Direct marketing using the Internet is the future – unless the postal service and telephone reduce their costs to near zero, there's no competition! Although this form of marketing over the Internet started off on the wrong foot – thanks to very heavy-handed marketeers who did not respect users' privacy – it is an effective medium that users are willing to accept.

Make sure that your marketing plans include delivery by email; many of your current contacts might even prefer to have material delivered by email. Once you have started creating parallel print and electronic mail-shots, you will soon find the printed version cumbersome, expensive and slow. Email marketing is cheap, convenient and immediate. Ensure that your methodology can use email now, or you will be the last on the bandwagon.

Newsletters are an alternative method of direct marketing. They combine elements of direct mail with PR and make a great service to your customers. A good newsletter takes time and effort to compile on a regular basis, but the production costs are near zero and you cannot be accused of spamming – but make it easy for visitors to subscribe. The combination of direct mail and newsletters ensures that your customers stay informed about your products, news and views. Best, they are relatively cheap and easy to implement and should be near the top of your online marketing checklist.

CHAPTER 8
Branding

PROMOTING a brand and image is just as important in the wired world as in the rest of your marketing activities. However, it is difficult to defend a marketing budget when compared to the direct marketing results that drive many of the commercial web sites. In fact, the suitability of the Internet for direct marketing and brand awareness has provoked many arguments on the web, to the extent that different supporters have produced presentations that promote each strategy. By using the Internet carefully, you can create and promote a strong brand image – in fact, you can create a 'virtual' brand that only exists on the Internet and has no real-world equivalent.

Internet Branding – the arguments

The arguments run as follows. Taking one stance, against the Internet as a branding vehicle, market-research has shown that the majority of marketeers do not consider the Internet suitable as a way of increasing brand awareness. It is too mass-market and geared towards selling and most companies are spending web-development budgets on sites that sell rather than sites that brand. The conclusion from one side is that the web is good for building sales and great for site loyalty – you're never more than a bookmark away from your favourite site – but not so good for brand awareness. Why advertise when web advertising is a waste of money, with viewing rates per banner ad higher than full-colour ads in a magazine?

The opposite view comes from other media companies that advise their clients, which the web is the perfect medium for branding. They provide excellent examples of large companies who have improved brand awareness through their web sites. With the deluge in shopping sites, most users want an information-rich experience rather than just a buying spree. As a result, companies that fit the profile should spend their web budget on banner advertising and a brand-awareness site rather than a complex shopping experience. You should advertise because web advertising is still seen as more credible than other forms of media advertising, such as television.

Internet Branding – the opportunity

Commerce on the Internet has begun to pay for the original development of large selling sites; these have fuelled the consumer interest and trust in buying over the Internet and make it essential to establish a strong brand. If you want to buy a book on the Internet, would you choose (or try and remember) the domain of a new start-up, or would you turn to established brands such as Amazon.com or BarnesAndNoble.com?

The good news for companies is that because the web is still developing fast, there is plenty of scope to create a powerful brand. With the information provided in this book, you can market your site, your company and your advantages with good effect. Choose your brand carefully and, with good PR, it's still possible to make a big impact on your web audience. Using other media, it would take more time, money and effort to move from start-up to recognised brand; the web, with its instant feedback provides an immediate reaction.

Reinventing your name

To create a strong brand, especially on the Internet, you need a good name. Your company name might be renowned to your customers, but is it easy to spell, is it short, does it grab attention and would it make a good domain name? Almost every successful brand on the web has a short, sharp and authoritative brand name that is the same as their domain name. Some, such as high-tech publisher Ziff Davis, have even changed the name to ZD to provide a logo and domain name with punch.

Every web site on the Internet is referenced with a unique domain name; even if your company has a registered name or trademark in the real world you will still have to re-register for a domain name. And if you are slow off the mark, you'll probably find that your preferred domain name has been taken by another company.

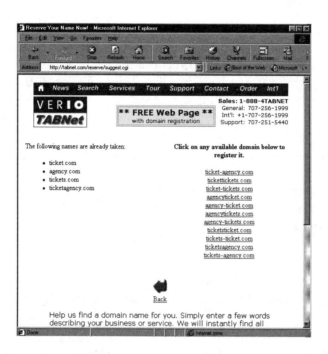

There has been plenty of publicity over the past few years about profiteers who register batches of domain names that have the same wording as a popular trademark. The idea was to re-sell the domain name

To give your company a more professional look, you should register your own company domain name for email and for your web site. For example, if you work for Simon's Ticket Agency, you could have an email address at CompuServe of 'TicketAgency@compuserve.com' but it is far more professional to have your own domain such as 'ticket-agency.co.uk' – your email address would then be 'simon@ticket-agency.co.uk' or similar. To register your own domain name is very easy – and relatively inexpensive. You can ask your ISP to do this for you or you can do it yourself by visiting the '*www.internic.org*' website. (Note that CompuServe and AOL users cannot have their own domain name, they will have to switch to an ISP.)

To complete this mini example, we would probably change the domain name for our company. The current domain name of 'ticket-agency.co.uk' is cumbersome and difficult to spell out – if you promote the brand 'Ticket Agency', users will not be sure whether to type in 'ticketagency.co.uk' or ticket-agency'. A sneaky competitor could register the similar sounding alternatives and gain advantage.

A neat example of this is with the mega search engine AltaVista. It's actual domain name is '*www.altavista.digital.com*' which is fine, but has allowed another company to register '*www.digital.altavista.com*' and '*www.alta-vista.com*' and so on. An example of the power of people that know the brand but cannot remember the address! As it happens, AltaVista is probably the best search engine and has millions of visitors who bookmark the site. However, compare this with the search engine Excite! Its web sites around the world are *www.excite.com*, *www.excite.co.uk* and so on - there's no mistaking the brand.

There are many examples of large corporations that have created a new 'brand' on the Internet by creating a new domain name. They started with their own company's domain name, but have split their web efforts into a neater web name that provides brand awareness and is easier to push as a branding site. If they sell goods, these are linked in via a selling site. Good examples include InfoBeat, Amazon and Pzifer.

InfoBeat (*www.infobeat.com*) started life as the Mercury Mail custom news service; it provides a great newspaper delivered daily by email to hundreds of thousands of readers. When the company started to provide third-parties with related services, it decided to change its name and increase the brand awareness. The old Mercury transformed into the cool InfoBeat; this name was promoted on banners advertising and links to related sites and it is now one of the top news information providers on the web.

Another example is drugs company, Pzifer. The company makes a range of pharmeceuticals, but it chose to create a branding site to provide information about its core products for the treatment of allergy. Instead of simply publishing a catalogue, or allowing users to buy sprays or eye-drops from an online shop, Pzifer chose to create *www.allergy-info.com*. This site provides a wealth of information about allergies, why they occur, how they can be minimised and ways of treating them. Visitors like the soft-sell approach and think of the Pzifer brand as a generous information provider.

Virtual brands, that have no relation to real-world buildings or shops, provide a new opportunity. Probably the best known (and so most successful) is Amazon.com (*www.amazon.com*). This online bookshop lists more than 2.5million titles and is, essentially, a selling site. However, Amazon have cleverly wrapped up the selling process within a great experience that's a joy for any book-lover. The company promoted the brand in banner advertising. One great feature was to create its 'associates' program in which any other site can link to the Amazon site and allow visitors to order books. The referring site earns a commission on any sales. The benefit to Amazon is that every associate site has a button that says Amazon.

Once you are on the site, there's no heavy sell. Instead, there are chat rooms, reviews, gossip and interviews with authors. Visitors can even add their own reviews to books. The key to their success is: if you want to buy a book, most people remember Amazon.com.

Provide Information

If you are trying to create brand awareness, make sure that your web site design and structure reflect the brand! If you are creating a selling site, you promote products, offers, prices. If you are creating a brand site, provide resources of information, involve the visitor with discussion groups, database access, feedback forms, and so on. Include support, help-files and background information. In short, make your site an experience to which the visitor will want to return.

If you want to sell from the site, make sure that the commerce features (shopping baskets, card authorisation, secure payments) are all in place and do not detract from the experience. I have often tried to buy something at a site, but been off because there was no secure server or the shopping basket was slow.

Software publishers and, to a certain extent, online booksellers have an ideal format for the mix of commerce and branding. You can visit the Amazon.com bookseller site and browse, read the latest reviews, chat to an author, check the top sales charts and more. Oh, and you can buy books! Software publishers, such as Adobe *(www.adobe.com)* have built a brand known for supplying graphics, design and image applications. If you visit their site, there are tutorials on design methods, sample images to download and trial versions of their applications together with support and updates for existing customers.

Advertise the brand

Once you have created your site, registered a memorable domain name and filled the site with information, interactive features and special offers, you can start to advertise the brand. (See Chapter 9 for more details on advertising.) By placing banner adverts on related sites, you can attract the attention of potential customers. Sponsorship of niche products works well – for example – sponsoring a newsletter or mailing list or information source works well.

Computer publisher O'Reilly is well known for its range of programming books about the Perl language – normally used to create actions behind the scenes at web sites. As well as its main site *(www.ora.com)*, the company sponsors the open Perl web site *(www.perl.org)* together with conferences and newsletters about Perl. It reaches exactly the right target audience and reinforces the message that the publisher is helping their community.

Conclusions

For many companies, brand awareness is an important part of the marketing strategy and budget. For web-based companies, branding is causing arguments over the medium – does it work or not. The answer must be that, yes, you can use the web for effective branding. You can also use the web to create a great selling site driven by click-throughs and viewer response. The two types of site are totally different in design and application and sit well together in the overall internet community providing users with information and services.

To create and promote your brand you need to move fast, since one of the raw ingredients, the domain name, is in short supply. Once you have your name, ensure that the site is well designed and carries the branding. Follow the suggestions in the rest of this book that cover the different aspects of branding and you will begin to create a successful site that is easy to access, informative and a well-known brand in its own right.

CHAPTER 9
Advertising on the Internet

WHEN a web site is popular, it provides a perfect vehicle for advertising – and site owners are only too aware of this. The most common form of advertising is to use banner ads – small rectangle-shaped images that are displayed on (usually at the top of) a web page. These provide a good way of promoting products and, if a visitor clicks on the banner, they will be whisked off to the advertiser's site.

The Internet provides both general and niche audiences on the same medium. If you want a general advertisement, you can advertise on a search engine site, such as Yahoo. Your advert will be seen by millions of visitors to Yahoo. If you want to target your advertising to a narrow band of users, you can advertise on a niche site or relate to the results from a search engine. For example, if you want to reach English teachers, you could advertise on the English teacher support sites or ask Yahoo to display your ad each time a user types in the keywords 'English teacher'.

Online advertising provides an exciting new market and outlet – it complements traditional advertising media and can reach niche targets very effectively. To cover the new technology, there is a new language of ad-speak, different rates and online ad agencies that buy or sell advertising on web sites. This chapter explains the different ways of placing an advertisement or selling advertisements on your site. I have covered the technologies and pricing models and compared the returns to those of traditional media.

Buying advertising on a site

Buying advertising space on the web is not hard – almost every web site will accept advertising, if you are prepared to pay for it. Web advertising has become another staple in the advertiser's arsenal of media – that already includes print, TV, radio and direct mail. If the product and advertisement are good and the audience targeting correct, then the results can be impressive.

The most popular type of web-based advertising is to use banner ads. These are low, wide graphic panels that you'll see displayed on almost every commercial web site. Unlike other advertising media, the size of the banner ads have become fixed into two main formats: 468x60 or sometimes 100x75 pixels.

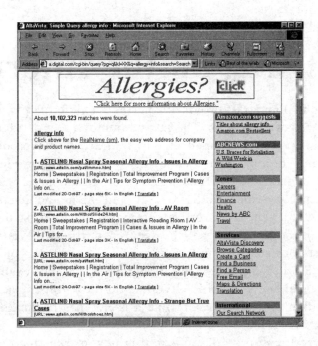

The two key terms to remember when buying or specifying banner advertisements are 'impression' and 'click-through'. When an advert is shown on a page to a user, this is called an impression. When an advert is displayed on a page and a user clicks on it and is transferred to another web page, this is called a click-through. When buying banner advertising space, you will be quoted one of three types of pricing structure that depend on the number of days, impressions or click-throughs (although, for small or first-time advertisers, only the first will apply).

Day rates

This is the simplest pricing method; your banner advertisement is displayed on a web page for a flat fee for a preset number of days. Some web sites will offer different rates to sponsor different parts of their web site and, in return, you get a masthead position at the top of each page. Other web sites charge to place your advert and advertorial copy (editorial copy written by you, the advertiser) on a special page.

Some examples of this service include the 'what's new' pages of many of the major search engines. You might think that this service is free, but it's actually bought up on a day or weekly rate. One of the most popular sites is Yahoo!'s weblaunch page. This provides a showcase for new web sites and allows a company to buy a slot in this section. Each entry normally consists of a screen-shot of the site, a short description and, perhaps, a banner advert. The flat rate to appear on the Web Launch site is $1000 per week.

CPM rates

The most popular pricing model for banner ads is called CPM (cost per thousand impressions). You will be charged according to the number of times that the ad is displayed on a web page. Typical costs vary from $20 to $200 per thousand times that your ad is displayed. To confuse matters, this pricing method is sometimes stated on a per-view basis – for example, $0.02/page view is the same as $20 CPM.

Banner advert management software makes automatically displays your advert in random sequence with other banner ads for either a pre-determined number of days or a pre-determined number of views.

CPA rates

The more exclusive pricing model for banner ads is called CPA (cost per action). You will probably only be quoted this pricing method if you have a proven per-view advertising record with the web site and if they like your product and think that it matches their customers. In this pricing model, you pay for each time that a user clicks on your banner ad that is hyper-linked to your web site. You pull the viewer from the original web site on to yours, lured by your banner ad. However, you have to pay a fee based on the CPA rate.

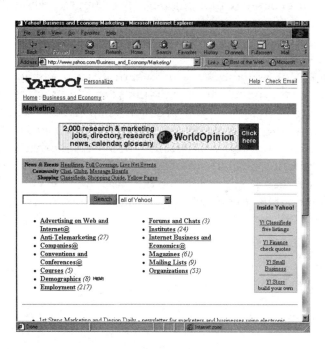

The usual method of upgrading to a CPA rate is to start with a standard, per-view charged model. If you plan to provide more focussed marketing or want to promote a particular item that needs further explanation on your site, you'll have to ask the site for a CPA rate.

Conversion rates

One of the key factors to bear in mind when buying ad space is the conversion rate between impressions and click-through rates. If your banner ad is shown one million times, what sort of click-through response should you expect?

When the web was young, a couple of years ago, surveys showed that the CTR of a banner ad averaged at just over two percent. For every 1000 times your banner image was displayed (called an impression), 20 viewers clicked on it and were transported to your web site. Times have changed, banner ads are everywhere and the users have shorter attention spans and suffer from information overload. As a result, current average CTR numbers halved to just one percent. New tricks help – if your banner has cool animated graphics, you can improve your CTR by 25 percent. Get the product targeting right and your CTR numbers can soar to 8-10 percent.

This depends, of course, on where your ad is placed. If you advertise in the general section of a general search engine (for example, Yahoo!) then you might get a 1-4% click-through rate. However, if you restrict your ad to areas of interest to your potential customers then you will get better rates of return. The downside is that this can cost more!

For example, one of the ways of ensuring that your ad is only shown to users interested in your product range is to link your ad to the search words entered by a user at a search engine. If you produce lampshades, your products would probably be wasted in the general section, but tie your banner ad in to keywords so that it is displayed when a user searches for 'lamps, lampshades, bulbs, lighting, home decoration, interior design' would ensure that your ad is seen by your core market. Most of the search engines offer this targeting service – called keyword links – but it often doubles the CPM cost of your advert to around $50-$60 CPM.

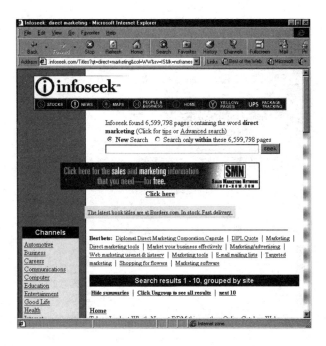

Some search engines and sites go further still and include customer tracking to narrow the profile of the visitors. For example, the InfoSeek *(www.infoseek.com)* search engine uses clever software to track the searches a user makes and builds a profile of each user. This can be used by the advertiser to provide a narrow criteria for selecting visitors. Similarly, sites such as Amazon.com *(www.amazon.com)* and other online book shops track the type of book or product that a visitor is looking for. This way, your advert for lampshades is only shown to visitors looking for books on lighting or interior design. This type of predictive modeling can improve click-through rates up to 10%.

Banner exchange cooperatives

If you are just starting out and have no budget for speculative banner advertising, you can still get your advert displayed on hundreds of other sites to thousands of potential customers. How? Use one of the banner exchange cooperatives, of which LinkExchange *(www.linkexchange.com)* is by far the biggest.

The service is simple: you register (for free) with LinkExchange and define the subject area of your products - from a list of over 1600 categories. You submit your banner artwork and, in exchange, include a special line of code in your web site. Each time your web page is displayed by a visitor, this line of code will automatically pull off a random banner image from the LinkExchange library (in the category that you have chosen) and display it on your site. The same thing happens on all the other sites registered with LinkExchange.

The drawback is that you have to carry advertising on your site, from a potential competitor. The advantage is that you will widen your customer base and reach new market areas – for free.

Published rates

To give you an idea of the current rates to advertise on well-known web sites, use the table below. I have listed some of the most popular search engine sites, simply because they are visited by the greatest number of people. The advantage of advertising on a search engine is that you can either opt for a general display to all visitors or you can use the visitor's search keywords to select when your ad appears (although this is more expensive).

Yahoo! search engine

Web Launch page	flat fee	$1000/week	includes short description, image and link to your site at the *www.yahoo.com/web launch page*
Banner advertising	CPM	$20 - $50 CPM	your ad is rotated with others in different sections or pages of Yahoo

Excite! search engine

Banner advertising	CPM	$30 - $60 CPM	for ad placement in a spe cific page ($30 CPM) or for display in response to a particular keyword search ($60 CPM)
General adverts	CPM	per impression	packages include 250K impressions for $6000 and 1m impressions for $24,000

Lycos search engine

Banner advertising	CPM/month	$20 - $50 CPM	general display of your ad rotated with others costs $20,000 for either 1m impressions or one month. Linking your ad so that it is displayed on a user's keyword search is $50 CPM with a minimum of 90 days participation

Netscape

Banner advertising	CPM	$17 - $25 CPM	display on a rotating basis on its popular 'what's new' page or quick start direc tory. This site is visited by millions of visitors every day, making it one of the most popular commercial non-search sites around.

Buying ads at auction

As an alternative measure to buy cheap ad space – although it's one normally taken to sell off excess ad capacity – you can use one of the online advertising auction houses. The ad spaces are listed by the automated auction system and the highest bidder wins. The prices are low – from around $1-$5 CPM – and give buyers a great way of getting cheap ad space and sellers a method of maximising every last ad slot on their site. The main online auction house is at *www.adbot.com.*

More information, prices and trends

Be sure to check the various sites to find the latest prices and conditions. It is also well worth visiting media buying sites and monitoring sites to find media agency buying services, trends and summaries.

www.doubleclick.com	one of the largest agencies that provides summary information for advertisers as well as media buying services.
www.ipro.com	large online advertising agency with background information, statistics and related links.
www.webtrack.com	trends in online advertising, sites used by well-known com panies and comprehensive information on sites that accept advertising.
www.marketmatch.com	lists popular sites that accept advertising and organizes them by subject areas and ad rates.

Designing banner ad media

When designing your banner advertisement, remember that you only have a small image in which to attract the reader's attention, so tell them about a product or service and tempt them to view your site. If your banner ad is boring, you are wasting your money.

The most popular format for banner ad images has settled to 468 pixels wide by 60 pixels high with a common maximum file size of 7Kb ~ the image must be stored in a GIF file format. Some companies specify other sizes that fit into their page design. For example, the Lycos search engine *(www.lycos.com)* limits you to banner ads that are 100pixels wide by 75 pixels high with a maximum GIF file size of 5Kb. In this space you can create any image that you want. Plenty of advertisers use animated images within this format to very good effect, otherwise make sure that you have a clear message, good design and a relevant product (the three simple rules of marketing!)

When creating your banner ad image, you will be advised by the web site managers how to format the image file. Most sites use a GIF file format – the standard used for most web-based images. This is simple to use, is compact and supports animation. However, if you need to reproduce photographic images, you will probably find that the JPEG file format, that has better colour support than GIF, is better suited. Check that the web site can deliver your JPEG format image before getting too involved in the banner's design. (See also Chapter 3 for more details on image file formats.)

Many web sites limit the size of the banner ad image file. For example, Excite has a maximum size of just 7Kb, whilst Lycos limits you to 5Kb. This is fine for a simple image, but will test your designer's skill if you want to create an animated image using the standard animated-GIF file format (that is also accepted for banner ads).

When designing the banner ad make sure that you use a professional web designer. Your banner is up against those from mega-spend companies such as IBM and Microsoft. A poorly-designed banner looks just that and can lose you visitors and wreck your image.

Because your advert is small, you need to pare down your message. Some of the important tips that are passed on by experienced banner designers are:

- make sure that your banner is at the top of the page
- keep the message simple and the words short
- don't try and describe the product – use a catchline
- a call to action boosts click-through
- pose a question to gain attention – but not too cryptic!
- make sure that the banner is relevant to the viewer – choose your media carefully
- don't over-use one banner design, change the design often (after 100,000 impressions for general sites)
- ensure that you direct click-throughs to the relevant product web page rather than your main home site
- use animation or bright colours to attract attention
- don't make it lewd or sexist
- make sure that you include your company name and web site even if there's a hyperlink
- use animation to show several different 'slides' that make the most of the image space
- adding the words 'click me' improves click-through
- 'Free' on the banner always works to improve click-through
- add a descriptive alternative text (using the HTML ALT tag) – over 10 percent of surfers opt not to view graphic images, so this ensures that your message is still seen (see Chapter 3 for more details on HTML commands)

Using alternative online media

Your scope for placing advertisements is not only limited to static web sites. There are several other online delivery systems that are relied on by millions of users. Find the right media for your product and a well-placed banner ad or sponsorship deal can work wonders.

Push technology and channel broadcasting

One of the neatest uses of the Internet has been the development of push technology, also called channel broadcasting or webcasting. This delivers customised news information to a user, that is then displayed either in a standard web browser or on a screen-saver. The user chooses the type of news, features, weather or industry-gossip that they want to receive and this is delivered to the user's desktop automatically regularly throughout the day.

Naturally, this free service is supported by advertising; it's a perfect way of getting your message to a narrow, targeted audience. If you are offering an online airline booking service, placing an ad in the travel report would be a perfect fit. The service is similar to traditional broadcast media in operation and pricing - although rates with each of the major push broadcasters are available only on request.

www.pointcast.com   one of the first and best push broadcasters around
www.netscape.com   develops its popular web browser and webcasting service

Newsletter sponsorship

Niche-subject newsletters provide an excellent and, normally, free service to interested customers. If you are interested in marketing, there are several monthly marketing newsletters that you can receive – including the excellent service from *www.wilsonweb.com*. These newsletters are several pages long and packed with interesting articles and news. The text is nicely formatted, often includes images and is delivered straight to your email box.

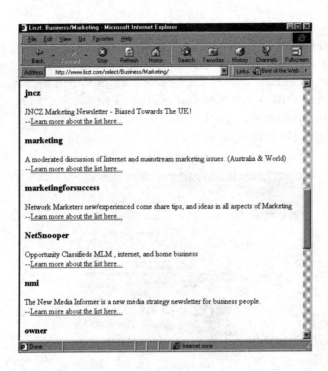

Newsletters are time-consuming to write each month, but do provide a valuable service to customers (see Chapter 7 for more information on writing and preparing newsletters). Because the newsletter covers a niche subject area, they are a great vehicle for sponsorship. For example, if you want to promote a new credit card for small businesses, sponsorship of a newsletter aimed at small-business people would ensure that your advert and message is delivered directly to the email box of the subscribers – people who want to read the newsletter rather than passive browsers.

Advertising in a newsletter is entirely down to the supplier. They might only want to advertise their own services or might be prepared to accept ads on a per-issue or per-subject basis. Visit some of the web sites offering information relating to your subject and see if they run newsletters. Try searching Yahoo! *(www.yahoo.com)* or Excite *(www.excite.com)* for suitable sites.

Newsletters are not the same as mailing lists – the latter is a method of distributing comments, information and questions between a group of users. There are hundreds of thousands of mailing lists (visit *www.liszt.com* to search for relevant lists) but you cannot advertise in them (see Chapter 7 for more information on marketing with mailing lists).

Usenet advertising

The usenet (that is made up of thousands of individual newsgroups) might seem to a perfect spot in which to advertise your products. Unfortunately, you should not. For a start, the messages you post are text-only and cannot contain images such as banner ads. Second, almost every newsgroup has a charter that forbids subscribers from placing blatant advertising messages.

There are ways of using newsgroups for marketing – rather than advertising – and I have covered these in detail in Chapter 5.

Electronic Coupons

Coupons? What has this often derided marketing tool got to do with online, cutting-edge marketing? Well, there is a great service that provides an electronic version of traditional printed coupons. You visit a central coupon site, check the area that interests you, download the relevant coupons, print them out and get a rebate or discount.

Two of the most popular coupon distribution sites are *www.coupon.com* and *www.ecoupons.com*. You can advertise on both sites within a particular, relevant section or you can place your own coupons online to get visitors to try your product with an initial discount offer.

Monitor feedback

If you are planning to place banner ads you must ensure that you have feedback and analysis tools in place. These will help you monitor the effectiveness of an ad at capturing the attention of a viewer and then keeping them on your site (although much of the latter will be down to your products and page design). I cover various ways in which you can check feedback in chapter 5.

However much you like your banner ad, much of its success will be down to matching the ad to the situation and type of viewer. Luckily, you can adjust your banner graphic as your campaign progresses to try out different designs. By monitoring the response of users to the different designs, you will find the best ad for this location. Unfortunately, there's no science about this – it's a trial and error process.

When you do monitor feedback, you can use an agency to monitor visitor traffic to your site or you can use standard access log analysis tools (see Chapter 5). To help you filter out the responses to your banner ad, create a new web page for these visitors – you will see immediately the response to this banner ad in the number of visits to your new page.

The key to banner ad feedback is to try and generate new leads or increase your customer base. Once a visitor has clicked on your banner and moved to your site, you'll need to try and convert this visit into a productive session. Ideally, you would like them to fill in a form with their name and address or register for new information. However, the conversion rate from click-through to registration is likely to be determined by the type of customer and the design of your site (see Chapter 3 for more details on design).

Comparison with print media

It's easy to get carried away with the idea of web advertising as the ideal media for advertising. However, there are plenty of sceptics who point out some painfully obvious lessons. Advertising in a high-profile magazine is expensive but the media agencies have calculated the following interesting figures.

Placing a four-colour, full-page advert in a magazine will cost you between $20-$40 on a CPM basis (using the number of readers and subscribers). Assuming that only two-thirds will actually see your advert, this increases the cost to between $30-60 CPM. It compare poorly with web-based advertising that charges from $20 CPM (although many specialist sites charge several times this rate). However, this is a passive view rate, not a click-through CPA rate. The bottom line is: would you rather pay for a small banner or, for a little more, get a large full-colour ad in a high-profile magazine?

Selling advertising on your site

If you have read the previous pages about buying advertising on sites, you might now be certain that the road ahead is paved with gold – if you sell banner ads on your site. Unfortunately, it's not quite true, but income from banner ads is a very useful source and can offset the costs of running the site.

In order to appeal to advertisers your site should have a niche focus. If an advertiser wants to reach a general audience, they can advertise on the general pages of a large search engine. However, your niche will be your key to reaching advertisers. For example, if you publish a site covering news, features and jobs for computer science teachers, then you have a potentially interesting, narrow audience profile that could be appealing to advertisers. If your site receives 30,000 separate viewers each month, you could easily claim that it served the majority of this market.

If a potential advertiser wants to reach computer science teachers, it could send a direct mail item to the teachers at their school – by renting a mailing list – or it could exhibit at specialist conventions. Your web site would appeal because it attracts this audience to it. If you do not mind including banner advertisements on your site, then you could cover your costs and, potential, make a modest profit.

To provide the potential advertiser with information, you would have to create a standard rate card, priced in CPM units (cost per thousand impressions or views of the ad). You would also have to provide auditing, reporting and control functions that would reassure the advertiser they are not gambling away their money.

Let's look at a potential business model for your web site. There are 30,000 viewers to your site each month. Because you reach a targetted audience, your rate card might be a little higher than a general site and look like this:

banner advertising	$40 CPM	for up to 30,000 impressions or for one month. The ad would be rotated with five others.
banner advertising per category	$45 CPM	for up to 30,000 impression open-ended. The ad would be placed in one of your specialist discussion pages,for example under 'jobs available'.

With this simple model you could generate $40 x 30 x 5 = $6000 per month for the five banner ads for your average 30,000 impressions. Add to this the couple of specialist subject forums that provide perhaps another $45 x 30 x 2 = $2700 per month and you can see that the potential annual income from your site is $104400.

However, selling banner ads is hard work. You will need to ensure that the software is approved and reliable. You must keep your site up to date and supply detailed visitor and click-through reports to advertisers. If you deal with media buying agencies then you will also have to pay them a 10-15% agency commission. Perhaps the best way to promote your space for sale is to include your site on a list run by a media buying agency such as *www.doubleclick.com, www.ipro.com, www.marketwatch.com* or *www.webmatch.com.*

There are plenty of extra, income-generators you could include in your web site. For example, if you include links from other companies, these could be charged at a modest fee of, say, $10 to include a link. It's actually rather cheeky to charge for this, but many companies are prepared to pay for link. If you run a newsletter or mailing list, you could offer sponsorship of both these products to a company. The rate you charge would depend on the number of subscribers and the frequency of the publication.

How to include banners
If you want to go ahead and include banner advertising on your site then you will need to buy and configure specialist software that can manage the complex process of displaying, rotating and auditing the display of banner ad images.

Banner ad management software
Banner ad management is a relatively complex subject that needs special software to operate. Firstly, a selection of ad images needs to be rotated so that each is shown on a regular or random basis. Second, a count needs to be kept of the number of times that the ad has been displayed. Third, a record of the viewer who saw the ad needs to stored using an access log. If you are planning to use more sophisticated visitor selection criteria, such as displaying an ad according to the subject displayed, then the management software will need to be able to handle this too.

The banner ad works from a line of code that is inserted into your web page file. This calls the management software – normally written as a Perl script – that will then decide which banner ad image to display. Some products use a cookie (a tiny file stored on the user's computer) to store details of when the user last visited the site and which banner ads they have already viewed to prevent duplication.

There are many ad management products available, some are freeware or shareware, others are full commercial products. The prices range from zero up to tens of thousands of dollars for very sophisticated programs. The best tactic is to assess the features that you want, then look at the various products available, with respect to their capabilities, support and ease of installation, and then their price. If you are prepared to do the installation yourself, you might find that a freeware product does everything you need. Alternatively, look at the commercial products which include installations and setup.

Selling ads using an agency

In the same way that high-profile magazines use media agencies to buy and sell their ad space, the online world has produced a number of agencies which can handle ad sales on your behalf. Some agencies charge a very high commission (up to 50 percent) of all sales and also pass on office running costs and expenses. Make quite sure that you know the full charge scale before your sign up. However, most of the agencies provide a very good service particulary useful for site owners inexperienced at selling ad space and who would rather leave it to a professional negotiator.

Visit some of the main agencies to see their services:

DoubleClick	www.doubleclick.com
SoftBank Media	www.simweb.com
WebConnect	www.worlddata.com

Selling excess ad space

If you sell ad space on your site and find that you have not filled every slot, you can auction off the remaining spots using an automated online auction system (mentioned earlier as a way of buying cheap ad space). The revenue from the auctioned space is minimal – between $1-$4 CPM – but it will ensure that you have a paying customer rather than an empty slot. The main automated online ad auction house is at *www.adbot.com*

Conclusions

There are many opportunities to buy banner advertising to improve the visibility of your web site or products. If you do not want to spend money, you could enter the LinkExchange cooperative or, if you do not have a web site, you could always use the electronic coupon system.

When buying ad space, try and get a narrow, targeted user profile. Some niche web sites can provide a far better reach to a niche audience than bigger, commercial sites. Just because the site is run as a hobby does not mean that it will not reach your prime audience (plus, it might be cheaper than advertising on a commercial site).

Placing banner ads on a web site is a good way of providing general promotion, but there are many other possibilities. You could sponsor a newsletter that is delivered direct to your target customer's desktop. Alternatively, try push channels or features of a web site.

If you plan to sell advertising on your web site, make sure that you have a full audience breakdown for your visitors. You will need to buy and install ad management software that can display ad images in rotation and count impressions. Lastly, you will need to audit the results and provide a fixed rate card that can be used by media buying agencies.

Online advertising has progressed over the past years and is now an established, recognised form of advertising. You can generate good responses for suitable products and, if you sell your own space, you can pay for the upkeep of your web site.

CHAPTER 10
Public and press relations

PUBLIC and press relations play a vital role in working with your customers and the media. The Internet provides a new, exciting way of using technology to help save time, effort and still improve benefits. By publishing a database of common questions and answers, customers can quickly solve a simple problem without waiting in a telephone queue; similarly, it saves you support staff. There are dozens of ways of improving the relations with your customers and giving them more information in an easily accessible format.

Dealing with the media provides another challenge; more and more reporters are now happy to receive news via email and, in response, there are several online news distribution agencies. Add an online library to your web site and include press releases, cuttings, reviews and other information – it helps journalists researching a story.

In this chapter, I have covered some of the different ways in which you can use the Internet to improve your relations – public and press. These ideas will help you provide better service to your customers and media and can save time, effort and money.

Public Relations

The one thing worse than customers complaining to the company is customers complaining to other potential customers. If a customer discovers that your product is faulty or that your service is poor, then they could complain direct to you – and we'll see how to encourage feedback later in this chapter. However, it's far more satisfying for the customer to complain in a public forum – but more damaging for your company's reputation.

The usenet – the collection of newsgroups – provides tens of thousands of different discussion forums in which anyone can say almost anything relating to the forum's subject area. I have covered ways in which you can use newsgroups to gain an insight into your customers' wishes and requests, but it is also worth remembering that customers can and do use newsgroups to complain.

One of your tasks should be to monitor the newsgroups and reply promptly and courteously to any complaints or problems voiced about your company. Having a running argument in public will serve no purpose, so try and settle and answer the complaint quickly and efficiently. If a product is really faulty, reply that you have passed this on to the product design department and manufacturing sections. Ask the key staff to add their findings to the newsgroup. This sort of immediate,personal response shows that your company is ready to listen to complaints and do something about it.

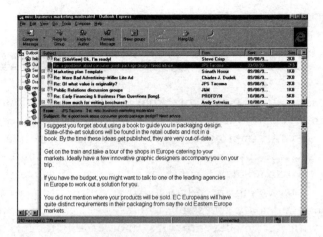

If there's a question about terrible service, post a 'I'll see what's happened' note and find out what was the cause as soon as possible. Reply and, if you are at fault, offer the user a replacement product. This might sound overkill for one user's complaint but, like consumer shows on TV, the newsgroup forums are scanned by millions of your potential or existing customers.

The practical problem is, of course, how do you listen out for complaints about your product? The best solution is to be a regular visitor to one of the newsgroup search engines. These index every message on every newsgroup and let you search for keywords - for example, your company name or product name. Visit *www.dejanews.com* or *www.altavista.digital.com* to search newsgroups.

When replying to any posting on a newsgroup, discussion group or other mailing list, do not overtly plug your company or your products. Try and provide unbiased, useful information or give your opinion. Make sure that your newsreader is setup with a signature file that contains your name, web site and company details – leave it to your signature to do the advertising.

Support

Many companies have to devote considerable resources – financial and human – to providing support centres for their products. Some staff will provide pre-sales service and advise potential customers on the best product; other staff will handle questions from customers about how to install, use or upgrade a product.

If a reasonable proportion of your customer base uses the internet, then you could work out a scheme to offer automated or email-based support. This has the advantage that, for non-urgent requests, you save staff time and costs and save telephone costs (especially if you provide a free-phone service).

The best place to start is to provide a FAQ (frequently asked questions) file. This contains a list of the most frequently asked questions about your products and suitable answers. Your support staff can provide a list of common questions of the 'my widget won't do this' style. Make sure that you keep the format and tone friendly and make it searchable; you can include all the information in a long web page and then, if it grows, structure and refine the document. Place this in a prominent place on your web site – typically accessed from a button next to your support number details (you want the customer to try and find the answer online before having to call your support staff).

From a simple FAQ, the next step could be what Microsoft calls a Knowledge Base. This is a database full of tips, ideas, solutions to problems and other tidbits about your products. This could be searched by customers online and would hopefully answer some of their more complex problems. Customers with a 'how do I get my widget to integrate with this' style question could find an answer given to a previous user stored in this database.

If you want to provide a customer-led environment, you could add a bulletin board or mailing list which allows users to ask questions. Some could be answered by your support or marketing staff, others could be answered by other users. See Chapter 3 for more details about setting up a bulletin board and mailing list.

Lastly, provide a direct email link to your support staff - try and use a personal or named email address rather than just 'support@mycompany.com' since this is hardly friendly. Ask your internet service provider to supply an autoresponder email account that sends an automatic message back to any sender acknowledging their support message and telling them that it will be dealt with in the next 24 hours. A good use of this system is provided by the Tabnet internet service provider *(www.tabnet.com)* which provides an electronic ticketing system. If you have a support query, you take an electronic ticket, enter your question and stand in line for an engineer to get to your problem.

Company information

It's well worth providing a company information page on your site – not just to boast, but to show that you're not an anonymous corporation. Include pictures of your office building – if it's elegant! – and images of key members of staff. Show visitors the structure of your company, how their questions or orders are processed and how the products are made.

Include a mission statement from your chairman or CEO and testimonies from influential customers who like your products. Explain why the company was started, its history and what it stands for. Assuming that you are not out to take advantage of your staff and customers then your customers will feel reassured by your company's open stance and, hopefully, confident enough to do business with you.

Try and provide personal email addresses for key contacts. If I send off an email to a general mail address, such as 'sales@mycompany.com' then I'm always a little unsure if it will get through. If I sent a message to the sales director, 'simon.collin@mycompany.com' then I would feel more confident of a quick response.

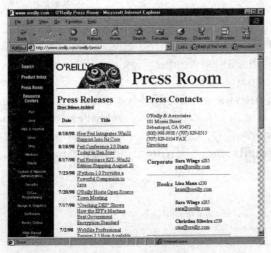

For public companies, provide shareholder information. Many quoted companies display the current share price together with the last company reports and news stories. These help boost shareholder confidence (and broker and financial confidence).

Updates

Use your web site to tell users about updates to your product range. The software industry has taken this to heart and normally provides update files online that can be downloaded by a registered user. The process is automatic so there are no support staff costs, telephone bills, postage or CD and disk costs.

If you manufacture a physical product, it's going to be rather more difficult to provide an update facility, but you should provide a page that tells your customers there is a new release available. For example, if you are a book publisher, include a new-editions web page to tell users that there's a new edition of a title. You could include a contents list, revision list and sample pages (stored either in plain text or scanned in as an image or Acrobat file (see Chapter 3 for more details on publishing information).

Ordering details

Since your web site is your shop window or stall, you should make it easy for users to request additional information. Include a simple registration form that allows a user to ask for a catalogue (some people still prefer paper) or request a sample or sales call. The responses to these registration forms will be automatically sent on to you by email (see Chapter 3 for information on forms); make sure that you follow through these mail messages. For catalogue requests, you could send an automatic response to confirm receipt and tell the user that the catalogue in on the way.

Interactive online events

One of the most popular new ways of providing excellent public and customer relations is online chat sessions. Many major sites have a schedule of online chat sessions in which any user can visit the site, start the special chat software and talk (via the keyboard) to an expert or panel. TV web sites feature well-known personalities as a draw to their chat forums, but you could include panels of experts or coverage of a specific use of your products. These are one step up from a FAQ or Knowledge Base and provide an immediate response to a visitor's question. See Chapters 3 and 6 for more information about setting up interactive online chat sessions.

Press relations

However strongly you feel about the power of the Internet, the majority of the public will still gain their information from the more traditional press, television and radio. However, you can use the Internet to offer better distribution of press releases, better contact with journalists and so build press coverage of your company and its products.

Reporters are using and relying on the Internet as a method of delivery and information. If a reporter wants to do a story on a particular product range, he can search the Internet to find all the (online) companies that provide this type of product, compare basic features and use technology background or white papers provided by each company to get to know the niche area. He can then look for research papers on university sites that cover forthcoming developments and, finally, look to newsgroups for customer feedback.

Press releases

One of the traditional roles of the PR or press office is to produce press releases which stir interest from journalists promoting them to write about the product launch, event or news. However, with so many press releases arriving each morning, it is difficult to even ensure that the journalist with an interest in the subject receives your release.

There are two ways of writing a press release for distribution over the internet: as a highly-formatted HTML file (the same commands that are used to create web pages) or as a plain email text. When storing your press releases on your web site to create your media library, use the HTML file format; if you are sending out press releases to unknown journalists, use plain text in a simple email format. True, many email programs now support formatted messages, but the majority of programs do not.

The online press-release

The Internet makes new demands on the writer of a press release but also gives them greater freedom. For example, you include hyperlinks to other press releases or background information within the electronic press release, making it considerably easier for a journalist to find all the related information. If you refer to your annual report, add a hyperlink to the report to make it easy to access. Similarly, by adding an email address (if you are formatting your press releases using HTML, add your email address using the 'mailto' command – see Chapter 3 for details on how to add this command) you give the journalist an immediate one-click way of sending you a question.

When creating your electronic press release, consider how it will be delivered. If you add image files to illustrate a product or person, make sure that these are small or, better still, separate them out from the press release and add a hyperlink from the main release to the image – giving the journalist the option to download the image.

Top tips for creating media-friendly press-releases include:

- use hyperlinks to link elements to existing reports, news stories or company profiles
- include email links for each contact person
- if the press-release is long, add a mini summary at the top with hyperlinks to the sections of the main document (saves scrolling) and repeat the contact details top and bottom
- separate out large images using hyperlinks to give the journalist the option of downloading the files
- store the basic details of your press release in a template web page
- if you are familiar with MS-Word or WordPerfect, use this to create your press release and export to the web-friendly HTML file format
- convert your existing press releases to HTML format (use the word processor's HTML export feature) to form a library of press information

Maintaining a mailing list

Email provides the ideal way of sending out a press release – it is cheap, fast, efficient and delivers direct to the journalist's desk. However, you first need to build up your mailing list of journalist's email addresses.

Look through your library of magazines to see if they have printed email addresses. Sometimes there is a standard guideline (for example, 'firstname.last-name@myMagazine.com') that is printed on one line. Newspapers are more difficult since they do not normally have a masthead but they do have web sites – check the web site and you will probably be able to find out the reporter's email address. Similarly with television and radio – the channel's web site often has a biography of each reporter and an email address. Many leading columnists and commentators have their own web sites - search for these using a standard search engine (such as AltaVista – *www.altavista.digital.com*). Of course, you can go offline and check your contacts' business cards or just telephone and ask for their email address!

Once you have your mailing list of contacts, add it to your email software's mail distribution feature. Most products – Pegasus, Outlook, Netscape, Eudora – all have distribution list features. Alternatively, many contact managers such as GoldMine and Act! have email distribution features built-in.

Distributing a press release

Your main email mailing list will contain the details of your personal contacts, but for general release you can use different systems to ensure that the release is delivered to every newspaper or press agency.

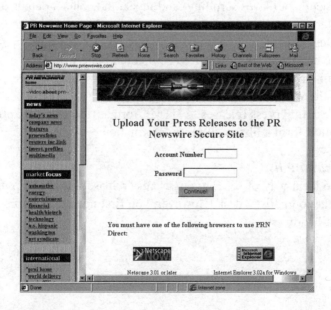

Commercial press release distribution companies (the two major companies are *www.businesswire.com* and *www.prnewswire.com*) distribute electronic press releases to online agencies – but charge for the service. However, these two services are now well established and can distribute your material to more than 2,000 media contacts and media databases.

There are several different distribution companies and each is good for different types of release. Some work only with email, others will distribute video clips, sound files and text. Some only work with particular types of product (for example, URLwire deals with web-based launch companies). The costs and coverage of each varies according to your requirements. The following table will help provide a better picture of how to choose your distribution service.

NAME	URL	COVERAGE	COSTS	SPECIALIST AREAS
BusinessWire	www.businesswire.com	email and publication to its online library	call	one of the major services widely used by PR and reporters alike
GINA	www.gina.com	email releases and pulication on to its web library	$180+	major distributor with excellent coverage of high-tech industry
Internet News Bureau	www.newsbureau.co	email releases and publication on to its web library	$225+	excellent coverage of different media, good for internet news
PRNews	www.newstarget.com	selects best-match contacts and sends email release	$100+	computer products service is core market
PRNewswire	www.prnewswire.com	email and publication to its online library	call	one of the major services widely used by PR and reporters alike
URLwire	www.urlwire.com	has thousands of contacts in specialist fields	$395-2000	specialises in web business launches rather than product launches
Xpress Press	www.xpresspress.com	email plus traditional fax, phone, letter	$195+	general computing business news

Answering press questions

In Chapter 7 I explained the role of newsgroups and mailing lists – allowing users to exchange information about a particular technology, product or job. These newsgroups are also widely used by journalists – they provide good feedback about a new technology, suggestions for features and help source case studies. For example, you might read a posting from a reporter asking how companies buy business travel; this could be used as a mini-poll to help the reporter get an idea of the market. By answering any questions, you will help the journalist and improve relations.

Some of the main press agency web sites (notably *www.prnewswire.com*) have online request forums. Reporters can place requests for information, review products and so on. Although this is a fee-based chargeable feature, it is a valuable resource when actively helping the media.

Conclusions

Managing your public and press relations is a vital role in any company. Good press relations ensure that your company's name and products are – at least – considered for inclusion in features, reviews and news. The internet has met the challenge with new enterprises that help distribute press releases to news agencies and key journalists – no printing, mailing or telephoning: the release is delivered direct to the reporter's desktop.

Keeping your customers informed is just as important; you can use the internet to help answer customer questions – with online conferences, answers to common questions and resource pages. You should not neglect the job of monitoring related newsgroups and mailing lists – your customers could be complaining about you or your competitors. These forums are more usually used to ask a question about a product, technology or query. Monitor the questions and, if it's your company's area of expertise, provide a useful answer – do not overtly promote your products, rely on your signature file to do this for you.

Top tips for online PR

- your PR plans should coincide with your web site going live
- make a list of your current contacts and their email addresses
- prepare a press release HTML template and convert past press releases into a web library
- visit other related sites, see if they have coverage from media that you have not targeted
- produce a 'press-office' within your web site to include company background,press releases, case studies, reporters mailing list and contact details

- use hyperlinks within online press releases to help reporters access related sites and files
- for wide coverage, use a press distribution service
- send personalised emails using your contact manager, email software or specialist program
- check magazine lead times and work accordingly – some major titles prefer months
- filter your releases by media requirements; some business titles do not print company or personnel news, others only do product reviews
- once you have sent your releases, try not to follow up with nagging emails – delivery is reliable and it gets to their desktop
- switch off the 'personalisation' features of some contact managers. For example, if your database has 'Andrew' some contact managers will try and be clever and use 'Andy' - use the formal name until you know otherwise

CHAPTER 11
Researching your campaign

PLANNING and researching your marketing campaign are crucial steps in creating effective publicity. The Internet provides the greatest source of useful reference material to help you research your campaign. There are government databases containing demographic information, telephone directories that providing business and personal names and addresses, marketing research papers, features on trends in spending, advertising and marketing, product news which has appeared in the media and, lastly, a vast library of user comments, requests and gossip.

The first step of any marketing campaign should be the research phase. Use the resources that are available on the Internet and you will have a clearer idea of your product's potential, the market opinion and information from any competitors.

One of the great features of the internet is that most of the statistical, background, news, and user-comment information can be searched for free. You will have to pay for some business-specific information (such as credit ratings for a company) but almost all the other sources of information are free to access.

Throughout this chapter, I will show you how you can make the most of this huge library of data and use it to provide clear background information essential for your successful marketing campaign.

Researching your competition

If you are working in a competitive sector of the market – and most are – then you will want to find out how your competitors are using online marketing to gain a business advantage. The obvious first step is to visit the competitor's web sites to see how they have organized their site and the types of information they provide. If you produce ornate lampshades, and your main rival has already set up a newsletter and mailing list from their site, is the customer base big enough to accept a second list or newsletter? Does the competitor's offering have a flaw or snag that yours could overcome? Have your competitors missed an obvious marketing tool that you could use to your advantage?

If your competitor accepts banner advertising, they might have a rate card published. If so, then they should provide visitor market analysis for potential advertisers – have a look at this to see if your site is doing as well. If the company uses an agency to handle all advertising, look at the agency site to see if this information is published – the main agencies include *www.doubleclick.com, www.ipro.com* and *www.marketplace.com.*

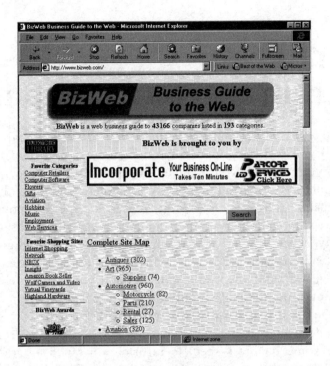

Many trade organizations include lists of links to web sites – your site might already be listed in a dozen different places without you realising. Here's a quick tip to search for all sites mentioning your site: visit the AltaVista search engine (it has the widest coverage of web site information) at *www.altavista.digital.com* and enter your web site's full address (called the URL) – for example 'http://www.myCompany.co.uk'. You will see a list of any sites that have links to your site.

You might be interested to see who is supporting a 'free' information site covering your market place. Perhaps you want to see if your competitors have already set up other web sites with a different domain name to their main site. Visit *www.websitez.com* to search for web sites listed by the companies owning the domain name.

What can you find?

The internet contains information on almost every subject you can imagine. Some parts are maintained by enthusiasts, others by companies. Almost all the information is free to search and display, but is covered by standard copyright law. The Internet provides three basic types of information source:

- the world-wide-web (www) made up of hundreds of millions of pages of information
- thousands of newsgroups providing forums for discussion on a specialist topic
- commercial databases published by companies, magazines and other organizations.

The main core of the Internet is the world-wide-web; this provides information available about airlines, financial organizations, governments, weather reports, sports results, reference and much more. Some information sources are linked to computers that update the contents every few seconds (such as a stockmarket status), other pages are static, such as annual reports or dictionaries. Many larger web sites include a search engine that helps find information on this one web site (for example, Microsoft's web site has thousands of pages; the internal search function works like one of the main search engines (such as Excite or AltaVista and helps you track down pages that contain the information that you want.

Commercial databases and archives are supplied by many large organizations and provide a valuable resource when researching media sources. For example, newspapers and business magazines often provide online archives which can be searched; financial companies publish historical share price information and company results.

How to search for information

The main way of finding information is to use one of the free search engines which index the contents of the web. These search engines are vast directories that try and catalogue every page within the world-wide-web – type in a search word or phrase and they list matching pages. There are dozens of different search engines and each will yield slightly different results (due to the way in which they each index the information). To get the best out of the web, use one of the new web sites or tools that submit your search query to all of the main engines at the same time – saving you time and effort.

There are many search engines on the Internet, many try and provide extra information to appeal to a particular type of visitor:

- Yahoo! *(www.yahoo.com)* provides a good, general-purpose index organised by category
- Excite *(www.excite.com)* is similar to Yahoo!, but uses artificial intelligence to try and find extra related topics.
- AltaVista *(www.digital.altavista.com)* provides excellent coverage of web page content and newsgroups
- InfoSeek *(www.infoseek.com)* similar to AltaVista in wide coverage of the Internet
- BizWeb *(www.bizweb.com)* covers business sites
- several engines provide UK-specific searching, including GOD *(www.god.co.uk)*, YELL
- Yellow Pages *(www.yell.co.uk)* and Yahoo!UK *(www.yahoo.co.uk).0*

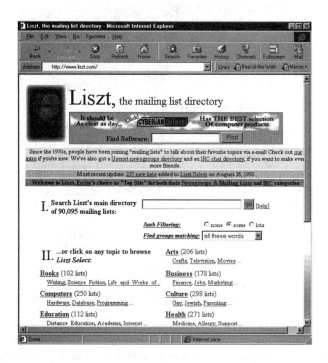

There are special search engines only covering the newsgroups, allowing you to find relevant discussion forums quickly. Each provides a similar services:
- DejaNews *(www.dejanews.com)*
- Liszt *(www.liszt.com)*
- Yahoo! *(www.yahoo.com)*, AltaVista *(www.altavista.digital.com)* and Excite *(www.excite.com)* are general-purpose search sites also covering newsgroups.

If you are trying to find someone's email address, try one of the 'white pages' telephone directories.
- Four11 *(www.four11.com)*
- WhoWhere *(www.whowhere.com)*
- Yahoo! *(www.yahoo.com)* and Excite *(www.excite.com)* are general-purpose search sites that also covering email addresses.

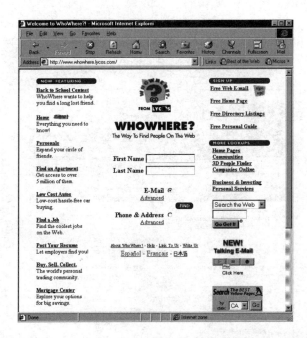

Make the most of your search time – use one of the search tools that will submit your query to all of the major engines at the same time. The results are collated and filtered for relevance.
- AskJeeves *(www.askjeeves.com)*
- Taxi *(www.taxi.com)*

Searching tips

Using the correct search technique can improve your chance of finding relevant information
- enter as many keywords as possible to refine the search (for example, search on 'coffee' and you will see a million matching pages; refine this with 'robusta coffee' and you will narrow the search field)
- refine your search further using the '+' and '-' symbols. Use the '+' to indicate that a word must be in the matched page and use a '-' to indicate that the word must not be in the matched page. Use these symbols just before the word, with no space between symbol and word.
- many search engines try and group pages by category. Try and use this feature to quickly find the correct category and then try a search. For example, under Yahoo *(www.yahoo.com)* select the 'Food & Drink' category, then 'Coffee' then search for 'robusta coffee'.
- the big search engines (Yahoo!, Excite and AltaVista) allow you to customise their opening page so that they show the categories that most interest you. Use this to save time when monitoring or browsing for new information.

There are many software programs which will automatically submit your search term to all the major engines at the same time. This ensures that you get the best coverage and that any old or out of date information is removed. Web sites such as the excellent AskJeeves *(www.askjeeves.com)* will submit your query to the major search engines (listed above) and then filter the replies; this helps you find relevant pages quickly and easily – although you might miss an interesting peripheral page. Some products, such as Taxi or Agentware, run on your computer and work with your web browser to help you find the information that you need.

For the ultimate in personal delivery, use one of the staffed search agencies. These people will take your query (such as 'find every news report about this company in the last four years') and provide exactly this material. They use just the same search engines but have extra filters and tools to help refine the data. Best of all, their services are relatively cheap and could save you hours of your valuable time.

Online newspapers and magazines

The Internet is an ideal vehicle for fast-moving business and financial information and provides vast historical resources. You can read a business story, research the company, read its annual report, check its credit rating and find its current share price from your computer.

Business newspapers, broadcasters and magazines provide good sources of current and historical company information; most services require registration but are still free of charge:

- *Financial Times (www.ft.com)* publishes all its news stories and company profiles
- *Economist (www.economist.com)* provides business concepts and comments
- Yahoo! *(www.yahoo.com)* and Excite *(www.excite.com)* and Microsoft Home *(home.microsoft.com)* provide custom business news services
- the BBC provides its news site *(www.bbc.co.uk)* with world and business news
- CNN *(www.cnn.com)* provides a US-centric view of world and business news
- Bloomburg *(www.bloomburg.com)* and Reuters *(www.reuters.com)* provide business news services – some parts are subscription only
- The *Daily Telegraph (www.telegraph.co.uk)* provides its complete text and back issues that can be searched
- *The Times (www.the-times.co.uk)* provides the complete text and back issues together with special features. The entire text can be searched.
- *The Guardian (www.guardian.co.uk)* and provides a cut-down version of its text
- The *Evening Standard (www.standard.co.uk)* provides the text of this London evening paper
- The *Wall Street Journal (www.wsj.com)* provides up to date business and financial news
- Reuters *(www.reuters.com)* provides worldwide news and features
- The Press Association *(www.pa.press.net)* provides hourly updates of world headlines
- ABC *(www.abc.com)* provides a rival service to CNN with an emphasis on features
- MSNBC *(www.msn.com)* provides world news with an emphasis on US coverage.

Financial stock and money markets are often a useful source of data for market researchers. You can find company reports, graphs of stock prices, broker quotes and recommendations at many of the main trading sites.

- *Financial Times*/Quicken *(www.ftquicken.com)* provides good overall information on personal finance and companies
- MoneyWorld *(www.moneyworld.co.uk)* provides links to a wide range of personal finance sites
- Yahoo! *(www.yahoo.com)* and Excite *(www.excite.com)* and Microsoft Home *(home.microsoft.com)* provide custom portfolio and share prices
- NASDAQ, NYSE, LIFFE and the UK Stock Exchange all have web sites with share price information.
- Many online sharedealing services provide extra information including historical analysis and pricing; ESI *(www.esi.co.uk)*, Charles Schwab *(www.schwab.com)*.

For news on appointments and profiles of business people, use one of the news gathering sites such as Reuters *(www.reuters.com)* or Press Association *(www.pa.com)* or Bloomburg *(www.bloomburg.com)*. You can also search for stories about people using the AltaVista *(www.altavista.digital.com)* site.

For budget, tax and government grant information search through the Government's own web site at *www.xxx.co.uk*. If you need export advice, the British Council *(www.britcoun.org)* has many background documents.

Searching News and Magazines

Use web sites that provide access to collections of newspapers, magazines and journals. This will give you an instant – and normally free – clippings library about any subject. One of the best free sites includes *www.crayon.com* which provides searches across hundreds of newspapers and magazines. If you want to extend your search to thousands of global publications, use a subscription service such as *www.lexis-nexis*.com or the CompuServe *(www.compuserve.com)* online databases which include ComputerLibrary (articles from computer press), Business Database Plus (articles from the business press) and Magazine Database Plus (general magazine articles).

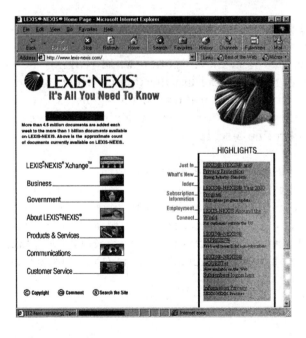

Getting information delivered to you

To receive regular bulletins of information you can subscribe to either 'push' channels or to broadcast mailing-lists. You can customise the service to provide only the information that you want.

- share price information for your portfolio can be delivered each morning via email
- keep up to date with business or industry news by subscribing to a 'push' channel such as Pointcast *(www.pointcast.com)* that displays current news within a screen-saver
- receive your customised newspaper each morning by email; general services include InfoBeat *(www.infobeat.com)*.

Pitfalls

Although the Internet is a very useful library, you should bear in mind the standard warning: there are a number of drawbacks and problems. Recognised publications and web sites will ensure that their material is checked and have excellent editorial quality control – other, smaller or hobby sites might not provide such stringent quality checks on the information available; this material could be biased or inaccurate. For example, it can be difficult to know if the information is proven or a wild idea from a student. You should really only base important decisions on information from well-known sources (such as newspapers, journal publishers or industry bodies).

The second problem is that you can easily spend more time trying to find a piece of information on the Internet than if you used your usual sources. This type of information overload is easily forgotten when judging the effectiveness of the Internet as a data source. Try and use the tips in 'How to search for information' (above) to refine your search or use one of the agencies that do the work for you; 'agent' software will search all the search engines or you can pay for a real person to carry out and refine a search.

Newsgroups are the new online notice board

Marketing as a theoretical exercise is a fine ideal, but the only way you can find out exactly how a campaign is working is to listen to the customers. Finding out public opinion is also a vital first step when researching your campaign and the Internet provides the perfect library of user comments, complaints and suggestions in the form of its newsgroups and mailing lists (these are covered in the next section of this chapter).

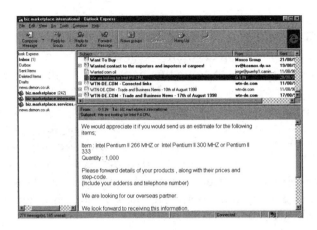

Newsgroups are the most popular part of the Internet and account for more activity than any other section. Newsgroups are an electronic form of a traditional bulletin board; anyone can enter a newsgroup and read previous messages or submit a new message. One of the interesting parts of a newsgroup is that it allows message-threads – groups of related messages. For example, if one person posts a new message asking for opinions on a new book, any replies would be linked to this original as a message thread. Anyone browsing the newsgroup can easily find and read the question and all the replies.

With more than 15,000 newsgroups on the Internet, there is coverage of just about every business, social and educational niche subject. If you want to know about high-school Spanish teaching or marketing for small businesses, you will find a newsgroup that covers the area.

To access any newsgroup you will need to connect to a newgroup server – almost all internet providers will provide access to the newsgroups (although some, notably the OSPs) will filter the newsgroups to remove offensive or pornographic material.

To read or submit a message you use a news reader program. Some web browsers, such as Microsoft's IE package, include their own separate news reader program. Other products, such as Netscape's Communicator, include a news reader feature built in. However, if you plan to work a lot with newsgroups you might find it easier to use a specially-written news reader product such as FreeAgent *(www.freeagent.com)*. This will help you keep track of new and important newsgroups, messages and replies.

Using a newsgroup for research

The messages stored in a newsgroup provide real-life reaction and questions from customers. Some newsgroups cover specific products (normally high-tech computer products) but other newsgroups will cover an area of interest rather than a specific product. By reading newsgroups you can get an immediate feedback about the customers' view of the subject, their likes, dislikes and requests.Start by finding the newsgroups that relate to your business area. In the same way that search engines index web pages and web sites, so other search engines index newsgroups and messages within newsgroups. If you want to search all newsgroups for particular keywords, you can use one of the main search engines covering newsgroup entries. Perhaps the best known is AltaVista *(www.digital.altavista.com)* which is normally used as a web search engine but also indexes newsgroups.

An alternative is to monitor a particular newsgroup. Your news reader will have a list of all the newsgroups available (new groups are added every day) and you can scroll through the list to find a suitable list covering your area. Check the new entries posted each day and, if you can, reply to as many as possible (this form of marketing is covered in Chapter 4).

Although you should not specifically post a message which sells your product, you can post answers to questions or other useful information and include your company's web site and products in a standard signature file (see Chapter 4)

Mailing lists distribute information by email

If you have not yet discovered mailing lists then you have missed one of the most important and interesting parts of internet life. A mailing list is really an automated method of distributing messages to a group of subscribers. For a public mailing list, anyone can subscribe by sending their email address to the program controlling the list. This program is normally called a majordomo or listserv (the name is always shortened from the expected listserver).

If any of the members wants to say anything or comment on a previous message, they send an email message to the mailing list's majordomo. Any message sent to the list is immediately re-distributed to all of the subscribers. Some mailing lists are moderated; this means that there's a team of managers checking all the messages submitted to the list to make sure they meet the list's criteria.

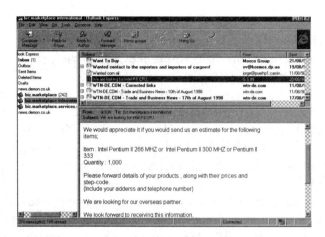

The advantage of a mailing list is that you do not need full internet access to be involved – you only need an email account. This makes it ideal for educational, government and business organizations providing email accounts for each user but not a news reader or web browser.

You should subscribe to the mailing lists covering your areas of interest. There are marketing mailing lists, lists on business on the Internet and lists covering your business' product area. With hundreds of thousands of lists available, finding the right list can be difficult. To help locate a suitable list, use one of the mailing list directories (or search engines) which store details of all the lists known on the Internet, what they cover and how to subscribe. Search engines include *www.liszt.com*, *www.four11.com* and the mailing list section of *www.yahoo.com*.

You can use the mailing list to see if anyone is complaining about a product – or your product – or asking for a particular service. You could also ask if members of the list would like to test a new product (but make quite sure that you do not advertise to a mailing list and follow the list's guidelines).

It's not difficult to subscribe to a mailing list and, if you wanted to, you could set up your own. All set up details are covered in Chapter 3.

Gopher hard to find information
The final, and rather elderly system of searching for information is called Gopher. Data files are normally tucked away in corners of computers linked to the Internet and, before the web took centre stage, these files were indexed using a system called Gopher accessed through another system known as Veronica. These tools provide a way of finding any file on the Internet ~ if you know the name of the file. However, since most market-oriented use of the Internet will be concerned with the content of the file, rather than the file name, these tools are not terribly useful.

Conclusions

The Internet provides a great research tool – if you know how to use it. It can provide background news and product reference, financial reports, geographic and census details together with customer feedback and competitor analysis.

However, this vast wealth of information is no help if you cannot find what you are looking for! One of the problems with the Internet is that many users are simply overwhelmed with the amount of information. There is no point spending hours trying to find information just because you know it must be on the Internet when you could do the same job by telephoning an expert. Don't waste time for technology's sake!

Much of the information on the Internet has been indexed and categorised and there are fast and powerful search tools that, if used effectively, can make searching quick and easy. Best of all, use one of the sites which submits your query to all the search engines at the same time. For the true custom service, you can ask one of the specialist search agencies to find the information you need. Send them an email request and their (human) operators will search and filter until they have the nugget that you are looking for.

To keep up to date, you can search newspapers, magazines, journals and other information sites. These provide a great way of finding press clippings and keeping up to date with relevant technology or products areas.

APPENDIX
Web sites

Research online
General-purpose Search Engines

AltaVista
www.altavista.digital.com

Excite!
www.excite.com

HotBot
www.hotbot.com

InfoSeek
www.infoseek.com

Lycos
www.lycos.com

WebCrawler
www.webcrawler.com

Yahoo!
www.yahoo.com

Yahoo! UK
www.yahoo.co.uk

Business-oriented search engines
BigBook
www.bigbook.com

BizWeb
www.bizweb.com

Magellan
www.mckinley.com

Yell
www.yell.co.uk

All-at-once search sites
Sites that submit your search item to top search engines, then filter the results. This saves time.

AskJeeves
www.askjeeves.com

Taxi
www.taxi.com

Searching Newsgroups
The main general search engines also index the contents of newsgroups.

DejaNews
www.dejanews.com

TileNet News
www.tilenet.news.com
Another good search directory that lets you find the newsgroup of your choice.

Finding mailing lists
Liszt
www.liszt.com

Finding People
Four11
www.four11.com

Yahoo!
www.yahoo.com

WhoWhere
www.whowhere.com

Electronic Mail
General-purpose electronic mail software

Qualcomm Eudora
www.qualcomm.com

Pegasus
www.pegasus.usa.com

Microsoft Outlook and Exchange
www.microsoft.com

Netscape Communicator
www.netscape.com

Email virus protection
Integralis MIMEsweeper
www.mimesweeper.com

Network Associates/McAfee
www.nai.com

Norton AntiVirus
www.symantec.com

Free Email services
(Almost all the major search engine sites offer free email, great for separating private and work mail.)
BigFoot
www.bigfoot.com

GeoCities
www.geocities.com

HotMail
www.hotmail.com

Microsoft Network
www.msn.com

Neat Email Tricks
Jfax Fax to email
www.jfax.com

Implementing autoresponders
(Your ISP should be able to provide a solution, alternatively use one of these products.)
AnsaBack
www.ansaback.com

AutoResponder
www.123promote.com

ReplyNet
www.reply.net

Direct marketing by email
US Direct Marketing Association
www.the-dma.com

Yahoo!
www.yahoo.com:companies:direct
marketing:email maketing

Direct email Management software
(Useful when sending large mail-shots.)

Arial Software Campaign and SignUp
www.arialsoftware.com

Colorado Soft WorldMerge
www.coloradosoft.com

MailKing
www.mailking.com

Alphasoft Net.Mailer
www.alphasoftware.com

ResponseNow
www.dbits.com

Renting opt-in email lists
Copywriter
www.copywriter.com/lists

EverythingAboutEmail resource site
www.everythingaboutemail.com

InBox Express
www.inboxexpress.com

PostMasterDirect
www.postmasterdirect.com

Targ-it
www.targ-it.com

Web Site Promotion
Tools to submit sites to search engines
All4One
www.all4one.com

Exploit
www.exploit.com

SubmitIt
www.submitit.com

DidIt
www.did-it.com

Information on search engines
www.searchenginewatch.com

Web award and what's new sites
(Most hi-tech newspapers and magazines also have top site guides, such as USA Today.com.) Yahoo!
www.yahoo.com/picks

Netscape
www.netscape.com

Internet Magazine
www.internet-magazine.com/sites

Infoseek
www.infoseek.com

600 award sites listed
www.resoluteinc.com/cyberonline/600 awards.htm

Web Response Tools
(Your ISP should provide access logs for your site, or use your in-house server's log files.)
Analog
www.statslab.cam.ac.uk/~sret1/analog

MkStats
find the nearest site with www.yahoo.com

Yahoo!
www.yahoo.com:internet:web:analysis software

Advanced visitor analysis
Accrue Software
www.accrue.com

Aptex
www.aptex.com

DoubleClick
www.doubleclick.com

GeoSys mapping
www.geosys.com

Intersé
www.interse.com

Advertising
Advertising agencies will buy and sell ad space

Advertising Agencies
DoubleClick
www.doubleclick.com

Ipro
www.ipro.com

Market Match
www.marketmatch,com

SoftBank Media
www.simweb.com

WebConnect
www.worlddata.com

WebTrack
www.webtrack.com

Alternative sources of banner advertising

Internet Link Exchange
www.linkexchange.com

Press Relations
Press Release distribution agencies
BusinessWire
www.businesswire.com

GINA
www.gina.com

Internet News Bureau
www.newsbureau.com

PRNewsTarget
www.newstarget.com

PRNewswire
www.prnewswire.com

URLwire
www.urlwire.com

Xpress Press
www.xpresspress.com

Creating a Web site
Web page design software

PageMill
www.adobe.com

Visual Page
www.symantec.com

Fusion
www.netobjects.com

HotDog
www.sausage.com

Frontpage
www.microsoft.com

HoTMetaL
www.sq.com

Programming resources

Perl programming language
www.perl.org

Java
www.java.com / www.sun.com

ActiveX
www.microsoft.com

Shockwave
www.macromedia.com

**Libraries of free/shareware scripts
and prgrams**
*These include hundreds of sample Perl,
C and JavaScript programs to enhance
your site.*

Builder.com
www.builder.com

WebDeveloper
www.webdeveloper.com

Freecode
www.freecode.com

Freescripts
www.freescripts.com

Image editing software
Adobe PhotoShop
www.adobe.com

PaintShopPro

Animation and multimedia
Macromedia Shockwave
www.shockwave.com

Link checking tools
(Your web page software should help find incorrect links on your site.)
LinkBot www.linkbot.com

Web browser popularity and compatability
BrowserWatch
www.browserwatch.com

Builder.com
www.builder.com

WebDeveloper
www.webdeveloper.com

Domain Registration
(Your ISP can register your domain name, or do it yourself with the main agency, InterNIC.)
InternNIC www.internic.net

INDEX